Words of Praise For...

Being Married: Secrets Women Wish They Knew

"WOW *Being Married: Secrets Women Wish They Knew* *is nothing short of BRILLIANT. It is everything that we wished our mothers had told us but didn't. AMEN to the truth of Laurie's wisdom. Packed with real-life examples of women who have been there, this book offers wisdom beyond ages. Anyone who is dating, contemplating marriage, engaged or even married already will glean years of wisdom from this little black book of secrets. This book should be a pre-requisite for all to-be-marrieds. Be the best friend you can be and pick up a copy for your sister, girlfriend, daughter, or even mother, step mother or mother-in-law! There is a lot of comfort in reading about situations that are more than relatable. Kudos to Laurie for her compassion, brilliance, and love of her fellow woman. An evergreen book, this work is a MUST READ! You can't put a rating on something this good, but if I had to rate the importance of this book, I'd give it 11 stars out of 10."*

—Sally Shields, *speaker, radio personality, publicity specialist and author of the #1 Amazon.com bestseller,* **The Daughter-in-Law Rules!**

"We love it! **Being Married: Secrets Women Wish They Knew** is undoubtedly the book that every woman should read before considering marriage—and even before entering into a serious relationship with a man. With the help of the women she interviewed, Laurie has covered in this book every conceivable topic that separates couples and leads to marital dissatisfaction, unhappiness and divorce. We highly recommend this practical, down-to-earth book and will suggest it as a 'must-read' for any single woman looking for a committed relationship."

—Susie and Otto Collins, *Breakthrough Relationship Coaches and Authors*

"If my clients had read Dr. Weiss's informative and resource packed book before they married, I might be looking for a new line of work!

Even if you think you know all about marriage and relationships, you are sure to learn something interesting and invaluable from Dr. Weiss's wise and intimate work. Easily accessible, the material is chock-full of useful and often surprising information.

Take advantage of Dr. Weiss's 50 plus years of marriage and over 40 years as a relationship therapist and marriage counselor. You will not be disappointed. A thoroughly engaging read."

—**Katy Kurtz,** *Denver divorce attorney*

"The words of wisdom ingrained in the wonderfully concise book by Dr Laurie Weiss are amazing. Somehow, Dr Weiss has been able to neatly package, without a lot of peripheral discussion, the most significant challenges I have personally experienced and have watched my friends experience as they live their married life. As someone who has been married and divorced, then married and

widowed, I can truly vouch for what Dr. Weiss presents here.

No matter how much in love you are or how disgusted you are in your current relationship, I highly recommend you read this wonderful book. **Being Married: Secrets Women Wish They Knew** *is a must read for all women, whether married or thinking of marriage ... it just may save you and your relationship."*

—Barbara Joye, *The Shift Guru, Author, The Creating Formula, Achieving the Life You Deserve*

"**Being Married: Secrets Women Wish They Knew** *by Dr. Laurie Weiss is the new manifesto for women. Whether they say 'I do' or 'I don't,' it's got all the ingredients for a woman to be smart, sassy, and successful. From demystifying the beliefs and myths of coupledom that detour so many; to handling money; and a myriad of unexpected hiccups, this book is a gem. The resources are excellent. It should be required reading for anyone single ... and it wouldn't hurt those who are married as well!"*

—Judith Briles, *The Book Shepherd*®

"Laurie expresses a wealth of information to women in all stages of relationship-life that can help them answer the question: Why does something that feels so good (a love relationship) become something that feels so bad? Backed by years of personal and professional experience with personal stories, her message is succinct and clear—on a psychological level everything has an explanation."

—Dr. Brenda Schaeffer, *Author,*
Is It Love or Is It Addiction?

"This book is an excellent resource for any woman, in a relationship or not. But, it is especially important information for a woman contemplating marriage. Weiss really gets at the core of what women need to consider before making that ultimate commitment."

—Kim Olver, *Author, Secrets of Happy Couples*

"In a world flooded with self-help texts, this book presents a well organized, thoughtful, and realistic 'guidebook' for a successful marriage. Moreover, sharing the 'secrets' of real

women makes it particularly enticing (delicious?). I wish I'd had a book like this years ago."

—Pam Gordon, *College Professor*

"Where do women most likely learn about all the ins-and-outs of how to build a healthy relationship anyway? Certainly not in the seventh-grade locker room or in health class. No one told us THE most important things to understand, relationship-wise and as such we presume that Prince Charming will love, honor, and cherish us till death do us part. WRONG! Relationships take work, understanding, and pro-active behaviors to make them stay healthy and satisfying. Helping women recognize that the fairy tale is not the truth, Laurie Weiss gives women the tools for making the right choices in a mate and whether or not marriage necessarily should be the end-all in every relationship. Unless you're a nun, every woman NEEDS THIS BOOK!"

—Mary Jo Fay, RN, MSN, *Author, Please Dear, Not Tonight: The Truth about Women and Sex*

BEING MARRIED

Secrets Women Wish They Knew

The Secrets of Happy Relationships Series

DR. LAURIE WEISS

Empowerment Systems Books

Being Married
Secrets Women Wish They Knew
The Secrets of Happy Relationships Series
Dr. Laurie Weiss

© 2019 Laurie Weiss

All rights reserved. No part of this book may be reproduced in any form or by any electronic or mechanical means, including information storage and retrieval systems, without permission in writing from the publisher, except by a reviewer who may quote brief passages in a review.

The author has done her best to present accurate and up-to-date information in this book, but she cannot guarantee that the information is correct or will suit your particular situation.

First published by The 99 Series 2012 as 99 Things Women Wish They Knew Before Saying I Do

Library of Congress Control Number: 2018950172
ISBN-13: 978-1-949400-00-7 Paperback
ISBN-13: 978-1-949400-01-4 Ebook
ISBN-13: 978-1-949400-02-1 Downloadable audio file

Published By:
Empowerment Systems Books
506 West Davies Way
Littleton, CO 80120 USA
Phone 303.794.5379
LaurieWeiss@EmpowermenSystems.com

Books may be purchased in quantity by contacting the publisher directly at:
Empowerment Systems Books
506 West Davies Way
Littleton, CO 80120 USA
Phone 303.794.5379
LaurieWeiss@EmpowermenSystems.com

Cover: Nick Zelinger, www.NZGraphics.com
Interior Design: Istvan Szabo, Ifj.
Editor: Donna Jara
Family & Relationships /Marriage & Long-Term Relationships/Self-Help

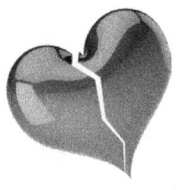

Dedication

This book is dedicated to: all the women who have so generously shared their lives with me—either directly or through their writings; my family, friends, teachers, mentors, colleagues, students, clients and readers; and most especially to the women who occupy two or more of those roles simultaneously.

Special Bonus

A 7-Step Process to Tame the Procrastination Monster and Learn to Negotiate

All you need to do is go to http://www.BooksbyLaurie.com/tame and claim your copy of this valuable guide that I refer to in several places in this book. I will happily trade it for your email address.

And I would be absolutely thrilled if you left a book review at http://www.BooksbyLaurie.com/BeingMarried when you finish the book. I'll give you more information about that later.

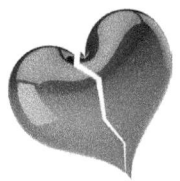

Contents

Words of Praise For… 1
Dedication 9
Special Bonus 10
Foreword 16
Introduction 18

Chapter 1: What You Should Know, but Don't 23
   You're Taught Expectations 25
   You Can Keep Your Own Identity 28
   You Can Grow and Change 29
   Connections and Expectations ≠ Reality 32
   He Can't Meet All Your Needs 34
   Address Disagreements 36
   Men and Women Really are Different 38
   The Golden Rule Can Kill a Marriage 40

Chapter 2: You Need to Know About You 43
   Others Tell You Who to Be 43
   You Try to Meet Expectations 47
   Waking Up is a Process 48
   "The Problem That Has No Name" 51
   You May Need More Education 53

You Can Ask for What You Want 56
You Have the Right to Say No 58
You Can Find Strength 60
It's Hard To Turn Off Your Programming 61

Chapter 3: Don't Hurry, Take Your Time 65
You're In Love—The Biological Imperative 66
Trying to Escape Rarely Works 67
This Isn't Your Only Chance 69
No Man Can Make You Whole 71
You Can't Change Him 73
You're Feeling Pressured 75
He Seemed So Nice… 77
You Think This Time Will Be Better 79
It's Okay to Wait 81

Chapter 4: Family Patterns are Important 84
Your Past Impacts Your Expectations 84
Each Family Has Different Rules 87
New Situations Challenge Old Rules 90
Different Family, Different Rules 92
Learn to Recognize His Family's Rules 94
Expectations about Following Rules Cause Problems 97
Codependency is a Cultural Expectation 99
Changing is Challenging 101
Recovering from Codependency 104

Chapter 5: You Don't Notice Very Important Things 107
Surprising Reasons for Choices 107
Looking Good Doesn't Last 110
Unconscious Choices Reflect Unresolved Issues 112
Conscious and Unconscious Agreements 114

Hidden Expectations Cause Problems 116
Notice Clues about Hidden Information 119
Those Not-So-Fatal Attractions 121
You Can't Make Him Change 124
Learning Together Works 127

Chapter 6: You Need to Discuss Your Values 130
Your Mask Won't Keep You Safe 130
What You Talk about Matters 132
Ask—Never Assume 134
Some Differences Really Do Matter 136
Defensiveness is Dangerous 139
Admitting Your Vulnerability Lets You Connect 141
Nobody Wins a Power Struggle 143
A Disagreement Isn't a Disaster 144
Communicating is Critical 147

Chapter 7: Physical Issues Take Attention and Communication. 150
Physical Attraction: Necessary But Not Sufficient 150
Physical Intimacy—Multiple Meanings 152
You Each Must Define Enough 154
Communicate about Sexual Problems 155
Sleeping Problems Interfere with Intimacy 158
Health Issues Can Become Critically Important 161
Affairs Happen When Problems are Ignored 164
Never Excuse Physical Mistreatment 167
Shocking Surprises Occasionally Occur 169

Chapter 8: Getting Married Doesn't Cure Bad Behavior 172
He Changed After We Got Married 172
He Doesn't Keep His Agreements 175
Abuse Must Be Named! 178

    Mental Illness is Frightening and Frustrating 180
    Alcoholism Causes Devastatingly Bad Behavior 182
    Marriage Isn't a License for Bullying 185
    His Priorities Don't Include Me 187
    He's Emotionally Unavailable... 189
    Should I Stay or Should I Leave? 190

Chapter 9: Stay Conscious About Money 193
    It's Best to Share Financial Responsibility 194
    Different Values Make Sharing a Challenge 195
    Sharing Responsibility Means Sharing Power 198
    Sometimes Deception is an Issue 200
    Lack of Skill Causes Problems 203
    Keep Your Own Financial Independence 204
    Learn to Communicate about Finances 207
    His, Hers, and Ours 209
    Planning Your Future Includes Retirement 211

Chapter 10: Spiritual and Religious Values are Important 214
    Definitions of Spirituality and Religion 214
    Spirituality is a Perspective 217
    Spiritual Value Definitions Differ 218
    Spirituality and Religion Help Explain Experiences.................... 220
    Spirituality and Religion Provide Community Support 222
    Differences in Values Create Tension 224
    Some People Search for Spiritual Engagement 226
    Selfishness Undercuts Spiritual Connection 228
    Using Marriage for Spiritual Growth 230

Chapter 11: Secrets that Make Marriage Work 232
    It Really Takes Hard Work 232
    Breaking the Codependency is Very Challenging 234

You Can't Complete Each Other 237
You're Two Different People..239
You Can't Make Each Other Happy...241
Disagreeing is as Important as Pleasing 243
Disagree Without Being Disagreeable...245
Trust and Respect are Critical 248
The Rewards are Worth It...250

Claim Your Special Bonus Now... 253
Please Help Me Reach New Readers 254
Acknowledgments 257
Useful Resources.. 260
About the Author... 267
How to Work with Dr. Laurie 270
About the Secrets of Happy Relationships Series 274
Books in the Secrets of Happy Relationships Series 277
Other Books by Laurie Weiss... 279
Stop Poisoning Your Marriage with These Common Beliefs....... 281

Foreword

As a certified CFLE family life educator and a parent educator for over thirty years, I'm excited about sharing Being Married: Secrets Women Wish They Knew It fills a hole that has needed to be filled for a long time.

Drawing on her own extensive experience and the wisdom of many women, Dr. Weiss offers a broad swatch of ideas to consider before saying yes to Mr. Right.

Learn to identify what can be strengths in a marriage and what can be stressors? What a gift! A rich buffet of ideas for a woman to notice, ponder, and take action on. Expect some surprises, for example, "Following the golden rule can kill a marriage."

BEING MARRIED

Engaging, encouraging, supportive, and gently challenging, Weiss' *Being Married: Secrets Women Wish They Knew* could help cut the divorce rate!

Before you say yes to Mr. Right, use this amazing list to pick up on things you may not have noticed. It could easily help you build a better marriage or avoid a heap of heartache.

Jean Illsley Clarke
Author, *How Much Is Enough?*

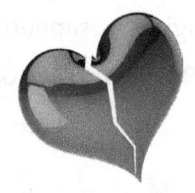

Introduction

Did you expect to grow up, get married and live happily ever after? Are you having second thoughts about that now?

Are you contemplating marriage and worried because in the US at the beginning of the 21st century more than half of all marriages end in divorce?

- Or maybe you've been married for awhile and you're beginning to wonder if the questions you have are normal or if there's something wrong either with you or with your marriage.

Being Married

- Or perhaps you are divorced. You've been married once or twice, and this time you are determined to make it work.

You're not alone. Hundreds of women who have shared their lives, their hopes, their dreams and their marriages with me have faced similar struggles. In over four decades of practice as a psychotherapist, marriage counselor and coach, I've been privileged to help these women face their challenges and move on with their lives.

I've used my experiences with these women, my own life experiences and my recent unscientific research to help create this book as a resource for you.

In gathering information for this book, I've asked many women to answer the question, "What is the most important thing you wish you had known before you were actually married? This can be about your husband, what marriage is like, health, history, yourself, expectations, families, children or anything at all." Women on my mailing list, women I've encountered at the local YMCA, women standing in line at the post office, women in a discussion group, women in a sewing circle, women attending parties and networking events—all have given thoughtful answers to this question, either face to face or via an online questionnaire.

More than fifty women have participated in this project. They range in age from their 30s to their 90s. Nearly 80% of them are between the ages of 36 and 65. They've all been married at least once, and 90% of them have at least one child. Surprisingly, women from eight different countries responded to my online questionnaire. Answers that came from outside the US and Canada were indistinguishable from the others.

I married a month before my 21st birthday and have been married to my husband for over 58 years. We're both relationship coaches and marriage counselors, and together we have spent over forty-five years studying, practicing and teaching relationship-building skills. We've focused our work on helping clients create dynamic, effective personal and working relationships.

Being Married

Our own marriage has often been our laboratory. Because we've worked together as psychotherapists, practicing and teaching in an international community, we've had unusual opportunities to develop an awareness of many things that enable people to discover the richness that it is possible to have in a long-term relationship. But it wasn't always this way.

Like everyone else, I grew up with a very limited view of what marriage could and should be like. My own parents maintained a traditional marriage for 58 years—until my mother's death. Before I got married it never occurred to me that I could or should know anything more about what to expect after I said "I do." Looking back, though, there are a lot of things I wish I had known ahead of time.

Almost every woman I've worked with throughout the years also needed the kinds of information the contributors to this project are sharing here.

I couldn't have done this book alone. Women who came from environments very different from mine shared issues I may not have thought to include. The things they wish they had known are not the same as those I have identified from my own experience and the experiences of my clients, relatives and friends. I'm grateful for the wisdom, eloquence, and broader perspective these women have brought to this book.

Most of the names of the contributors to this project have been changed to protect their privacy. A few of the women have given permission to be identified, in which case both their first and last names have been included.

I hope the secrets shared here will make your journey easier and richer.

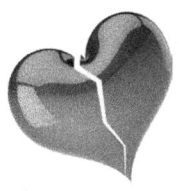

Chapter 1
What You Should Know, but Don't

*"I wish I'd known what marriage is really like—
instead of swallowing all those myths about marriage."*

Two Don't Become One

When asked what she wished she had known before she got married, Maria answered, "Nothing—I was good to go." When you're young and in love, you too may think you're good to go. You might not be. It depends upon how much you're going to try to make yourself and your marriage measure up to the mythical ideal.

Renee tried! When she started really looking at why she was so unhappy, she realized that she believed it was her job to give up what she loved and embrace what her husband loved in every area of their lives. She just could not live up to her own ideal of what it meant to be a wife.

If you try to constrict yourself into half of who you are in order to become the wife you think you're supposed to be, you may end up surprising yourself by:

- exploding over something simple
- starting to fight frequently about everything and nothing
- getting depressed
- losing interest in making love
- finding someone else so attractive you wonder if you've married the wrong man

There's no way to know ahead of time exactly what your marriage is going to be like. You have ideals and fantasies based on the marriages you observed when you were a child and what the media has taught you about marriage. Your real learning will come from experience, from the day-to-day reality of creating your life as a married couple.

You're Taught Expectations

Michelle says, "I wish I had been told it's not the happily-ever-after fairytale—that it's a 24/7 job of taking care of everyone else, and you come last. He works 9 to 5 and expects you to have dinner for him."

Have you ever wondered how the myth of living happily ever after became such a part of our reality? Perhaps it came from the Disney movie where you saw the prince ride up on his white horse and rescue the heroine. Maybe you learned about relationships from the romance novels you read when you were in high school—or from equally unrealistic movies, social media and TV programs.

When you were a child, you lived in a magical world and had little opportunity to learn what a real relationship might be like. If you had the good luck to live in a healthy, functional family, you were probably shielded from the normal struggles of the adults. Even if you did notice grownups struggling in their relationships, you probably thought that yours would be different: you simply wouldn't have those kinds of problems because *you* would marry "the right person."

By the time you started to have "practice" relationships as an adolescent, you were relying on your friends—your all-important peer group—to determine the right way to behave. And they had the same kind of misinformation that you did. It's nobody's fault; it just happens that way. You grow up both believing in and rebelling against stories about who you are supposed to become.

What you bring into a marriage depends upon your age, as well as upon your life experiences. When you marry, you and your husband can bring both complementary and competing myths into the relationship. Complementary myths are often more evident when you first fall in love: they help to make the relationship "feel right" because you are fulfilling each other's unspoken expectations. One of those expectations may be that your marriage will be like your courtship, only better.

You may believe that there will be less stress and more happiness as you relax into your roles as husband and wife. Unfortunately, this is not always true. Marriage itself changes the character of a relationship, and not necessarily in ways you would expect. Even if you've been living together successfully for some time before you actually make the commitment to marry, the early programming about what marriage is like is activated by taking your vows.

You then struggle to enforce agreements you think you have made with each other but probably have never discussed. Of course, if you were lucky enough to have had premarital counseling, you may have been a little ahead of the game. Even so, most people simply try to do what they think is right, and then they struggle without even knowing why.

You Can Keep Your Own Identity

Janelle says, "I wish I'd known that it's absolutely wrong to do things you don't want to do just because your husband or society expects you to do something, or to be something or someone they want you to be."

Constance, who raised five children, wishes she had known "that marriage and children can cause a dangerous loss of personal identity." And Jennifer, who is married and has two young children, didn't realize "how much of myself would actually become spent for the benefit of others."

When you try to turn yourself and your husband into that mythological "one" you may think you are supposed to become as a married couple, you may assume you have to give up anything about yourself that your husband doesn't like. In exchange, he is supposed to fulfill all of your emotional needs. Of course, neither one of you can keep this bargain, although you may exhaust yourselves by trying to do so.

Ultimately, you'll need to set aside these myths in order to figure out what kind of marriage you really want to have. You can't do it by yourself, and you can't do it by trying to mold yourself into what you think your partner wants you to be. It doesn't happen magically. It happens by having conversation after conversation with your spouse about how you can best do each of the things you've dreamed of doing together.

You Can Grow and Change

Both you and your husband can to continue to grow as individuals, within your marriage. This is very possible, and it does take work.

Edith wishes she had known "that women could honor and love themselves and not depend on the man to complete you." Donna wishes she had known how to love herself more so she could be treated with respect.

It may be a challenge to find support for becoming a separate and valuable person. Lucky women get help from other people who are already doing this. Help can come from friends, from relatives, from support groups, or from a therapist or counselor. It can even come from your husband. My husband and I were fortunate enough to stumble into the emerging world of the human potential movement that was storming California in the late 1960s.

Transactional Analysis was our gateway. We learned about the Games People Play, and we started to climb out of the boxes our families and our culture had taught us were the only way to live. We became passionate about helping others emerge from their boxes–mostly because we wanted to be in a community of supportive people.

Being Married

Fortunately there are far more opportunities for women to develop themselves now than there were in 1970. However, it's still true that learning to love and respect yourself doesn't happen all at once. It needs to become a lifelong practice.

The word *practice* here is important. A practice means it's something that you must consciously choose to do. It's not something you learn once and have in your repertoire forever. Athletes and artists must continuously practice in order to stay proficient, and so must we.

Over the years my clients have sometimes been disappointed that they could lose the changes they made when they allowed themselves to go back to their old ways of thinking, feeling and behaving. If you want to live as a conscious human being, it really is a lifelong learning process. You may start out hesitantly and painfully, but the more you practice, the more fun and fulfillment you'll experience.

Connections and Expectations ≠ Reality

Morgan says, "I had many unspoken and not-conscious expectations. I felt like I needed to fit into a role that I had seen modeled, and I expected my husband to fit that role also."

Be careful about making assumptions—especially about yourself, your husband, and what your marriage is going to be like. If you think about the word "assume" as "ass-u-me," it may help you remember that when you make an assumption, you're in danger of making an ass out of you and me.

If you don't avoid making assumptions, you may *assume* your marriage will be traditional, a lot like your stay-at-home mother's. You may *assume* that you'll both work and share everything. You may *assume* that you'll live happily ever after.

You may be like Melissa and assume that you are the only responsible person in the world. Even though you have a full-time job, you may assume that it is also your role to be fully responsible for the household, the grocery shopping, and the childcare. Because many men still have that assumption about the role of the women they marry, you are very likely to find and marry one of them, especially if you are like Melissa.

Your husband may say he will share responsibilities, but his assumption about what that means is probably quite different from your assumption about what it means. Assumptions will get you into trouble every time. They are definitely not a substitute for conversations.

Many of the women who answered my questions shared that their marriages didn't match their expectations.

- Gretchen said, "It isn't a 50-50 deal. I do most of the work at home."

- Janet admitted, "I made an assumption of reciprocity and didn't notice that there wasn't any."

- Several others said, "It didn't turn out to be the traditional marriage I expected."

Susan summed it up by saying, "I would've liked a more realistic view of what living with someone was like."

When your expectations aren't met, you may be unhappy, and now you realize why. I was angry at my husband without really knowing that I was angry. Actually, after a while, I was just angry at my life but not aware that I had any other options. I had no clue that my hidden emotions were affecting my behavior. They did, and that probably had something to do with the reason my husband suggested that we see a therapist. I was lucky.

He Can't Meet All Your Needs

Several women wrote about starting marriage believing that their husbands were supposed to fulfill all of their needs. Conversely, they all expected to be able to meet all of their husband's needs. And in fact, during the falling-in-love stage of a relationship, it's natural to have your lives completely revolve around each other.

BEING MARRIED

However, after the honeymoon stage is over, things change.

One person simply can't provide everything another one needs. We're just too complicated. Even one adult has difficulty fulfilling all of the needs of an infant, and as the child grows, it takes more and more people to create a stimulating and growth-enhancing environment. Adults are many-faceted and continue to need all kinds of stimulation to stay engaged in the world.

Over the years I've often worked with marriages that were crumbling because one or both partners had chosen to shut down those parts of themselves that they couldn't engage with their partners. Like me, when I thought I had to give up listening to the music I loved because my husband didn't like it, they were dying on the inside and blaming their partners for their misery.

Amy expressed it this way: "I wish I had known that a husband cannot fulfill all emotional needs – that maintaining friendships is the key to satisfying long-term emotional stability." Linda adds, "I wish I could have known that one person would not be able to fulfill my needs for emotional and intellectual stimulation."

Address Disagreements

Rachel says, "I wish I'd known that the hardest thing about the first five years of marriage is learning to adapt to each other." Adapting generally means actually identifying and talking about differences as they come up, but many people find it very uncomfortable to have those conversations.

There are a lot of different ways to not have those uncomfortable conversations about disagreements.

- You can simply not notice that they exist in the first place and assume that your spouse sees the world exactly the way you do.

- You can gloss over them and pretend they don't really matter.

- You can notice that they exist but experience them as so overwhelming that they seem insolvable, so you decide it's better to just ignore them.

- You can notice them but feel so inadequate about managing any kind of conversation (or confrontation) that you sincerely believe there is nothing you can do about them.

When disagreements aren't addressed they may fester and explode, or they may go underground and lead to one or both of you withdrawing emotionally, losing interest in your physical relationship and just going through the motions of being married. And that's just the beginning of the list of the negative consequences of ignoring disagreements.

Helping my clients and my students learn how to have those important conversations has become the focus of my professional life. I've included several resources in the appendix that will help if you need to learn to say what you think without getting into trouble or hurting someone else's feelings.

Men and Women Really are Different

Besides those major differences, there are many different personality styles. The problem is that on some level, we all believe everyone experiences the world the same way we do.

No one really knows exactly how much gender differences are influenced by biology and how much by our environment. Hormones, especially estrogen and testosterone, direct our behavior in subtle ways that are not fully understood. Research has demonstrated that males are more motivated by having an impact on their surroundings, while females are more motivated by relationships.

Women tend to pay more attention to feelings than men do. When something distresses them, they often want to tell someone else about their feelings. They aren't hoping for the other person to solve the problem or make them feel better—they just want to share what they're feeling with someone who will empathize with them. The problem is, if you tell your husband about your distress, he is likely to immediately suggest ways for you to solve the problems that created the feelings in the first place. You'll probably get angry because he doesn't understand that you just wanted to vent and because you didn't get the empathy you wanted. He'll probably be confused or angry because you're not accepting or appreciating his efforts. He may even feel ashamed because he's been ineffective in solving your problem or making you feel better, and that will make him even angrier.

On the other hand, men don't necessarily have ready access to their feelings. In a workshop for couples, Peggy told her husband Nick, "I want to know how you feel about this." Nick replied, "I'll be glad to tell you, but sometimes it takes me a few weeks to figure out how I feel." Most of the other men in the room nodded vigorously.

Of course, not every couple fits this pattern: some women are more focused on solutions, and some men are more relationship-minded. If you would like more information about personality style differences, you can check references to the Enneagram, the Myers-Briggs profiles, or the Personal Profile System.

The Golden Rule Can Kill a Marriage

When your spouse scratches your back in the place that his back itches instead of in the place where your back itches, something feels weird. You know he's trying to do something nice, but somehow you don't fully appreciate it.

Because you think your husband is just like you and he thinks you're just like him, you try to be nice to each other by giving each other the things you want for yourselves. You may even do this to try to communicate to your husband that he should give you what you are giving to him, and vice versa. This can be very confusing to both of you. It's bewildering to give someone exactly what would make you happy, and then to discover that not only did you fail to please him, he is actually angry at you for what you did.

Here's what it looks like in real life. My husband and I stopped holding hands with each other shortly after we were married. Many years later, we were astonished when we found out why we had stopped holding hands. When he held my hand, he would rub it continuously. I like my hand held firmly, so when he would rub mine, I would grab his and hold on tight. But he likes to have his hand rubbed, so he would break loose and rub mine some more. We were each trying to signal what we wanted by giving it away. It didn't work, and we didn't even notice the pattern until we learned this principle.

Kelly suggests a great resource to learn more about this: "I wish I had read Gary Chapman's book, *The Five Love Languages,* prior to getting married. It would certainly have helped me to understand my husband's love needs, and I think it would have helped me to explain why I was upset and felt unloved when he didn't pitch in enough. In my mind, this is a book every couple should be required to read before they get married. Their lives would be so much better and the divorce rate would plummet."

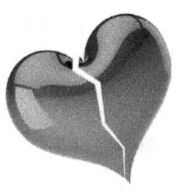

Chapter 2
You Need to Know About You

"I wish I'd known more about myself."

Others Tell You Who to Be

When you're a girl, learning to be a woman, you get lots of advice about how you're supposed to act and what you're supposed to be when you grow up. But do you recall anyone ever telling you to pay attention to how you felt or what you wanted to do? That may have emerged gradually, if you had the time and if you were lucky. I was one of the lucky ones, so I had some wiggle-room that many women don't get.

Young women still eagerly seek instruction from social media aimed at teenagers, and sometimes from their mother's magazines as well. You absorbed these instructions too, until you just knew you were supposed to be a wife. Did you read the articles and posts that offered instruction about how to find a husband and what to do with him after you land him?

Your parents and your church (or synagogue or mosque) also give you instructions. My parents assumed that I would go to college, find my future husband there, graduate, and then get married. Yours may have assumed that you would marry your high school sweetheart.

Sometimes those assumptions are reinforced deliberately, sometimes accidentally. When I was raising my own children, my father proudly told me, "We never said *if* you go to college, we always said *when* you go to college." On the accidental side, hearing a sarcastic "Just who do

BEING MARRIED

you think you *are*?" can have a devastatingly negative impact.

In their attempts to help girls find career paths, school counselors have often made inadvertently limiting suggestions. These limits were based not only upon an assumption that most girls will marry and thus not need a permanent career, but also upon the belief that women are unsuited to many types of jobs. The helpfulness of any counseling you received was probably dependent upon when and where you went to school. Even today, many young women are advised to think of traditional service jobs instead of opening up to the entire world of possibilities, especially high-paying career options.

Sylvia's aptitude testing suggested a career in medicine, which her school counselor interpreted for her as "nursing." She says, "I didn't want to be a nurse, so I took the other obvious choice for women at that time: I became a secretary. Eventually I became a secretary for doctors, when what I had really wanted was to *be* a doctor."

And if you were exposed to the fairy tales of the Disney movies, you may harbor a secret belief that Prince Charming will come along and you will get to be a princess—and, eventually, a queen.

But no matter where the programming comes from, it comes from outside you. Because it surrounds you, you absorb it without thinking about it at all. And even if you are privileged like I was, you may still be discouraged from stretching and testing yourself.

One professor suggested that I avoid the more difficult advanced coursework because, after all, I was just going to get married. I was already un-officially engaged, so I accepted his suggestion.

I had more choices than many of the women my age who grew up expecting to become wives as soon as they graduated from high school—or even sooner if they happened to become pregnant. Regardless of our circumstances, most of us adapted to the instructions and expectations of others.

Being Married

You Try to Meet Expectations

You're a good girl, so you do everything you know how to do to earn the approval of everyone you meet. "Everyone" includes your family and your extended family and your neighbors and your schoolmates and your teachers and your best friends and your boyfriends and their best friends and their parents and your employers and your rabbi (your minister) and the clerk at the grocery store.

That's a pretty extensive list of people to please. In trying to please them, you have to learn to pay close attention to the various subtle signals they send, and you can spend a lot of time agonizing over what those signals mean. I certainly did, and so did most of the women I have worked with.

With so much energy focused on paying attention to other people's signals, there's very little time or energy left to notice what you might want or need. Many women have told me that each time they expressed anything about what they felt or they wanted, they were criticized for being selfish.

With all that pressure it's no wonder that you don't get to know yourself very well. What self? Did you even have one? The only self you knew was the one that was busy trying to squeeze into the molds built by other people. It's no surprise that a full 10% of the women who helped with this book told me in one way or another, "I wish I had known myself better."

Waking Up is a Process

Waking up doesn't happen all at once, and it usually starts accidentally. You're innocently minding your own business and you stumble over something that suddenly (or gradually) shifts your perspective on your world.

Sometimes it's a lot like Alice in Wonderland falling down the rabbit hole. Women help each other through the process. A friend or neighbor sees your plight and says something or invites you to do something new, and you're off!

Being Married

- Walking away from an automobile accident that could have killed her changed Linda Lee's awareness and perception of almost everything.

- Attending a yoga class she chose because child care was available changed Judy's career path.

- Marilyn attended a class at local junior college. The class, entitled A Woman's Life, opened her eyes to new possibilities.

- Krista attended the same class, became aware of her own isolation, and started reaching out to others.

- Terry took a class called Life after Divorce. It shifted her awareness of the impact she could have with others.

- A couple of chance conversations with other women started me on an exciting journey that continues to expand my life almost 50 years later.

My wakeup call came when I was 29 and introduced myself as Jonathan's wife. A young woman replied "I am a person in my own right." That startled me. Two years later I had lunch with an ardent feminist who told me, "You're not free." I answered, "I certainly am! My husband lets me do anything I want to do." Duh! After hearing myself say this, even I couldn't escape the truth: my words had demonstrated my belief that I needed permission from my husband to make choices.

Even with that kind of awareness, it isn't always easy to make changes—especially if your husband and your family feel threatened by them. They are afraid they will lose the benefit of having your life revolve around them as you start to explore your own wants and needs. It often takes a group of determined women to support each other's growth.

That is how I started my own growth process. I spoke about my experience with friends and colleagues. We started having coffee once a week and taking the risk of sharing our deepest dreams with each other. We all started supporting each other in making the new choices that have helped us achieve things we never even imagined were possible.

"The Problem That Has No Name"

In 1963, researcher Betty Friedan published a book about a strange phenomenon she observed: Women who apparently had everything were discontented. College graduates doing everything they were expected to do in their lives found that it just wasn't enough.

Friedan identified this discontent as "the problem that has no name," which is also the title of the first chapter of her famous (or infamous) book, *The Feminine Mystique*. The problem she was observing in the homemakers of the 50s hasn't gone away. It has changed form and become the lament of the working mother or the corporate manager, women who are getting ahead by following all the rules and are exhausted by the daily grind and the rising expectations. Now each longs to have more time for herself and to spend with her husband and her children.

Sometimes this working mom is a professional: an attorney, doctor or CPA who has had years of training to allow her to practice. Now, frustrated and exhausted, she asks herself, "Is this all there is?"

It's not about what you're doing, it's about making a conscious rather than an adapted choice to be doing it. It's about tuning in to that little voice that says, "This is what is real and important at this stage of my life."

Listening to that voice of truth can be scary and disconcerting. It may tell you that past choices of husband or career path no longer fit. Acting upon it may mean risking losing everything you think you value—your family, your economic security, the respect you enjoy in your community—yet if you don't act, you feel like you're slowly dying inside.

It doesn't have to be an either/or dilemma, but because you are trained to follow rules you may not have the negotiating skills, the support, or the confidence to take a stand for yourself. It would be easier to shut up the voice and pretend that you have never heard it

I tried that once. It worked for a while until I got so depressed I didn't want to get out of bed. That got my attention, and I felt enormous pressure to change everything. I was terrified! I don't have space here to tell you how I did work it out. The entire story is told in my book, What Is the Emperor Wearing? Truth-Telling in Business Relationships, which is about learning to tell your own truth without getting into trouble. You can read about it in the Resources section or at http://www.BooksbyLaurie.com.

You May Need More Education

Sometimes you just don't know how little you know. Paula shared this advice: "Wait until you know yourself." Then she added, "But at 20 I knew everything."

When you are desperately trying to establish yourself as an adult, it is completely understandable that you don't want to listen to the voices that say, "Slow down, take time to learn." But it's not too late!

When you think to yourself, "I can't! I don't know how!" stop and ask this question: What exactly don't I know? How can I learn how? Who do I know that does know how? Will she teach me?

Even if going back to school is far too big a step, you have almost infinite resources available to learn almost anything you want to learn. If you're near a public library or own a computer or a Smartphone you can find instructions for doing hundreds, perhaps thousands, of different activities for free. All you have to do is search for them on YouTube. My insatiably curious 12-year-old grandson taught me this trick.

When I Googled "best free college courses online" I turned up over 89 million results in a fraction of a second. Try it yourself and see what appeals to you. You can't get college credit, but you can learn whatever you want to know. Your employer may be of help, too. Ask!

And even if math terrified you, there is hope. You can go step by step from about 3rd grade through calculus and beyond, for free and in private, at www.KhanAcademy.org. There's lots of other material there, too.

Ask your friends and neighbors also. Don't you feel flattered when someone comes to you to learn to do something you consider incredibly easy? Almost everyone does. My neighbor was happy to teach me how to roll out piecrust, and I am happy to teach people where to find resources for publishing their own books—and lots of other things. One caution here: respect professionals who earn a living by teaching people how to do things. Some professionals are happy to answer brief questions, but they do charge for their professional services.

You Can Ask for What You Want

Dolores says she wishes she had known she could speak up about what she wanted. I wish I had known that also. Like many women who don't know they are allowed to speak up, I had other strategies to try to get what I wanted from my husband without asking. You probably know the drill also.

Your first strategy might be to hint. You talk about how much you admire something and how nice it would be to have it, and if that doesn't work, you might try whining about not having it. Then you might try giving him what you want, hoping he will notice and give it back to you.

When we were first in business together, I tried to drive the business in the direction I thought it should go by pushing Jonathan ahead of me and pretending he was the leader. That was a really bad idea.

You have to do a lot of unproductive manipulation when you don't know that you have the right to ask for what you want.

Being Married

On the other hand, asking for what you want can seem to be very risky. What if he says no? Or, even worse, what if he gets angry about being asked? It can be embarrassing when you have exposed your vulnerability by asking for what you want, and then the other person refuses your request. That's especially true if you've spent years being a good little girl who was taught to be polite and hope someone would notice her and give her what she wanted.

It may take some effort and experience for you to realize that *not* asking for what you want is riskier than asking: if you don't ask, you're a lot less likely to get what you want than if you do ask and allow the other person to know what would actually please you.

Asking for what you want is the first step of the negotiation with someone else who also has desires that may or may not match yours. It's also important to recognize that if you don't get what you ask for, you are in essentially the same position you were in before you asked: You didn't have it then, and you still don't have it. You're better off, however, because you have gained information. It is now clear that the other person is not willing to give you what you want, at least under present circumstances. This frees you to either negotiate or find other ways to meet your own needs.

You Have the Right to Say No

Linda says, "I wish I knew how to be comfortable saying no." Author and counselor Linda Lee Landon teaches that "'No' is a complete sentence." It is not necessary to justify or explain or attain agreement about your refusal.

Many women have been trained from childhood that it is just plain wrong for them to ever say no. Instead, fearing to take the risk of actually saying no, they either say or imply that they will do something even when they don't want or intend to do it. Then they either deliberately don't do it or they tell themselves they intend to do the task but somehow never get around to it.

One way of acting out the "no" you feel inside, but aren't willing to say aloud, is by procrastinating. You can say no by putting off doing something you agreed to do, either for someone else or for the taskmaster part of yourself. You may make yourself feel guilty for not doing the task, but by procrastinating you get to put it off for a long time, and you may even avoid it altogether because you have missed a deadline.

In my practice as a psychotherapist, I have known many people, both women and men, to make enormous life changes just from the practice of giving voice to the part of themselves that has been forbidden to say no at all. They practice saying "No, I don't want to …" in private many times a day. Then they do a follow-up program to integrate what they don't want with what they really do want. You can learn more about the "Learning to Say No" program in your special bonus, *A 7-Step Process to Tame the Procrastination Monster and Learn to Negotiate.*

We each need to learn that we are separate from everyone else in some ways and connected to them in other ways. Saying no is a really important activity for establishing your own personal boundaries and maintaining your own integrity. Integrity in this case means "wholeness" as a separate human being.

Saying no is also an ultimately kind response. Most people would rather know that a particular door is closed so that they can seek other opportunities, rather than waiting and hoping (and continuing to annoy you) for something that is never going to happen.

You Can Find Strength

You may be avoiding doing something important because it would mean taking a risk. And the possibility of failure seems overwhelmingly scary. You may have little confidence that you could actually succeed, but you may be underestimating yourself.

Melissa, a 30-something divorcee, wishes she had known about her ex-husband's mental health issues. But she also says, "I wish I had known that I am strong enough to have two full-time jobs, study for a degree, and bring up a child, all at the same time."

Phyllis dated many different men before settling down with her second husband. She reports, "I wish I had known how strong I can be and how much I could accomplish once I set a goal."

These are just two of the stories of what strong women have managed to do when they tested themselves. There are many more.

That doesn't mean to take risks without thinking them through and setting up an appropriate support system. Think about your options. Think about what you want. You may be a lot stronger than you think you are.

It's Hard To Turn Off Your Programming

Sadly, just knowing yourself isn't enough. It's an important first step, but we all have deeply ingrained patterns and habits that we developed as children, simply because we're human. We all learn to adapt to our parents or caretakers and the situation we find ourselves in when we're small.

Once we believed we understood what our lives were supposed to be like, we all put ourselves on automatic pilot. Unless you rediscover your story by getting to know yourself, you will still tend to follow the rules you set for yourself a long time ago.

Judy shared: "When I got married I didn't really know who I was, what I truly wanted from life, where I was going or how to get there. I was functioning well on the surface, but it wasn't until I was in my early 30s that I began to remember my childhood.

"I knew I had been adopted, but I did not know I had been abused by my birth father. So when all of that came to the surface, I went through a long period of depression, self-hatred, man-hating (including my husband), questioning everything about my life, and many suicidal thoughts. It was not a pleasant couple of years, to say the least.

Being Married

"I always wondered why I reacted to things the way I did, and it wasn't until after these memories came out, and years of counseling and therapy, that I realized I had been suffering from PTSD and these suppressed memories were the cause of my physical pain.

"Had I known all this earlier in my life, my marriage would not have had to go through the many stages of 'hell' that it did. Thank goodness for a man who stuck by me and encouraged me to get help. My husband is a real example of what love is all about."

It takes time and work to dismantle the automatic pilot and live your life the way you choose to live it now. Even when you do, the automatic pilot still shows up and tries to take over when you're not paying attention.

After 58 years of marriage, almost 50 of them spent consciously learning and growing, I still find myself slipping back into some of the traditional and comfortable patterns I thought I had given up long ago. Instead of fighting them the way I used to, I ask myself what purpose they are serving in my life now. Then I can decide whether or not to keep those patterns.

Sometimes resurrecting an old pattern is a sign that my new way of dealing with things is not working in a particular situation. If I discover that I have fallen back into the old pattern because of an unmet or unrecognized need, I can ask myself whether there is a better or more direct way of getting that need met. Often there is.

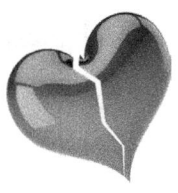

Chapter 3
Don't Hurry, Take Your Time

"I wish I had known I didn't need to be in such a hurry and could take the time I needed."

JoAnn said: "Be careful who you trust—time tells all. Don't be in a rush to move forward in the relationship—the longer you can wait, the more you will learn about the individual." However, many women find reasons for acting too quickly.

You're In Love—The Biological Imperative

Being in love is a fantastic experience. Your focus is completely on the one you love. You wear blinders, seeing all the ways in which you fit together and none of the warning signs about your differences. Being close is the most important thing in the world.

You know that you are just perfect for each other and will fight anyone for your right to be together. In short, you know EVERYTHING! But you are under the influence of powerful forces beyond your control ….

Nature wants babies. Your genes don't care about anything but reproducing themselves. That means your hormones may be more in charge of your decisions than your mind is. Hormones live in the moment. There is no past and no future— there is only right now!

In short, you are suffering from temporary insanity. The best thing you can do is enjoy the ride and know that you are in no condition to act on decisions you might want to rethink when you are sober.

And remember to protect yourself sexually, both from unknown diseases and from nature's whims. Although a wise friend once told me, "Don't sleep with anyone you would not want to share the rest of your life with," I think that is difficult advice to follow. Waiting might be best, but it may be hard to do; so for now, use protection and avoid getting pregnant.

Just remember those powerful forces beyond your control…

Trying to Escape Rarely Works

Suzanne, married three times, shares this advice: "There is always time to make the right choice. Never be in a hurry to marry out of fear of loneliness."

If you were raised in an alcoholic, abusive, neglectful or other severely dysfunctional family, you are desperate to escape. You may see marriage as a convenient way to do so. Unfortunately, you may be jumping out of the frying pan and into the fire.

You may leave a bad situation only to discover that you have chosen (or accepted) a man who is much like one of the abusive parents you just escaped. Often that discovery comes as a rude awakening when you have children and are completely economically dependent on your abusive spouse.

In any case it can take a very long time to escape from the abusive relationship.

Not all escaping women marry abusers. If you marry a nice, ordinary man and simply can't seem to connect emotionally, you may feel like you have made a mistake. In this case counseling, either individually or as a couple, can dramatically improve the situation.

During the time you are leaving a bad relationship, you are especially susceptible to falling into another. Taking your time the second time around may be even more important than the first time.

Being Married

This Isn't Your Only Chance

Cynthia, divorced, shares: "I wish I had received wise counsel of a spiritual and psychological nature as a preparation for marriage. If I had had sufficient self-esteem I believe I would have waited longer to find someone who was a really good match instead of marrying the first kind man who asked me (out of my desperate loneliness).

"However, I do see this now as a journey/destiny I had to undertake and that good will eventually come from this as I turn these experiences into compost for the work I want to train to do—art therapy with the dying. An easy life would not have given me the experience and compassion that this choice of career will draw from me. For the first time I finally have a sense of something worthwhile to do and for which I can make a real contribution- better late than never."

Thinking that this is your only chance is often one of the reasons a woman marries quickly to escape abuse. Living in an abusive family and low self-esteem fit together.

After all, when you are continuously told that you are to blame for all of the bad things going on around you, it is easy to conclude that they (parents, siblings, other relatives) are right. You may even decide that there is something very wrong with you.

Some conscientious girls even reach this conclusion for themselves. They believe this: "I should have fixed things, and because I didn't, there is something wrong with me."

Girls who do not meet conventional standards of beauty, girls who are different in any way, or girls who are bullied at school for whatever reason also decide that "I am the problem."

Once this belief about yourself is set, usually when you're still a child, it is hard to change. You have "low self-esteem" and consider yourself unworthy of good things. So when a man, any man, shows you attention, you are both thrilled and afraid. You are afraid he'll find out about "the real you" and you're afraid he'll get away. Of course you are tempted to hurry!

Being Married

No Man Can Make You Whole

Catherine, divorced, says: "I was so unhappy and emotionally abused. I wish I had known my own worth and that it was okay to not to get married unless I was absolutely sure that my partner and I were right for one another. I was lonely—I thought I needed a man to make me whole."

Fairy tales, most traditional children's stories, cartoons, adolescent romances, internet content, movies, TV, etc. surround most of us from birth onward. Although these stories now feature girls who are braver and more resourceful than the ones they portrayed in the mid-20th century, they still show most of those girls longing to find a husband. Heterosexual couples are the norm, and it is hard to imagine any other possibilities.

The destructive myth of two becoming one is rampant. It's a great spiritual concept, but in the real world it becomes an excuse to not develop all aspects of yourself. Instead, you expect your partner to add the missing parts.

That myth leads to the belief that you NEED a man to make you whole.

And, as a Lesbian woman pointed out, sometimes a man really doesn't fit in the picture at all.

Needing is not the same as wanting. Remember, you're biologically programmed to reproduce. That does require a man—or, at least, his sperm. Cloning is not included in your programming. And you probably do WANT a man, for a variety of obvious reasons. But there is no need to hurry.

Judy wishes "someone would have told me to enjoy my life more: smile more, do 'silly' things, read books in the sun, take naps, daydream."

Marriage works best when it is between two complete people. Take the time to develop yourself before you take the plunge.

Being Married

You Can't Change Him

You can't "marry the man today and change his ways tomorrow."

This lighthearted refrain from the award-winning 50's musical Guys and Dolls was heard on Broadway again in 2009. The expectation that you can get someone to change for the better after marriage persists despite a ton of evidence to the contrary.

If you hear yourself making excuses for the man you hope you'll marry, take this point very seriously.

It doesn't take much to change from:

> "He loves me so much he wants me to spend all my time with him." to

> "He gets angry when I spend time with my friends." to

> "He blames everything that is going wrong to my listening to my friends." to

> "I have to sneak around to see my friends and my family." to

"He says I'm a bad person because I want to see anyone else." to

"I think I'm going crazy, but I'm afraid he will kill me (or kill himself) if I try to leave."

Bad behavior usually gets worse. Other unfortunate excuses I have heard include:

"He only acts this way when he has a few drinks."

"He is really, really sorry that he hit (pushed, shoved,) me, and he has been so nice since then."

"He says he really needs to spend lots of time with his friends at the bar."

"He just looks at porn to relieve his stress because of work (the wedding, the race, etc.)"

These are all warning signals. There are lots of others. If you encounter them, as our Colorado mountain road signs say, "Don't be fooled, there are steep curves ahead!"

BEING MARRIED

You're Feeling Pressured

Catherine shared: "I remember wanting to break up with Bob very early on but feeling guilty because he was more into me than I was into him. I wish I had known that after marriage I would feel 10 times more trapped and stuck than I felt before marrying him."

Three thoughtful women between the ages of 46 and 55 spoke clearly about the impact of going through with weddings they knew, on a deep level, should never have occurred.

This wish comes from a woman who is still married and did not share her name. She says, "I wish I had known how important it is to believe your own intuition. If I did, this marriage of 16 years would never have happened."

Dana, long after the end of her 22-year marriage and in a successful long-term relationship with another man, echoes her: "I wish I had listened to my inner voice the morning of my wedding and called it off then."

Suzanne, now into her 3rd marriage, warns, "You should not get married if you have ANY doubts or second thoughts...especially strong ones."

Intuition is information about the world that you perceive in a subtle way that doesn't match the language you normally use to interpret and report on your experiences. Sometimes the best way you can express it is as a funny feeling or a gut feeling that something unusual is happening. It is almost like a message from a usually unnoticed part of yourself that is being sent to your conscious mind.

Scientists have only recently been able to measure brain resonances that apparently are connected to these subtle ways of experiencing the world. But just because we can't measure something very accurately does not mean it doesn't exist. It does exist! It is real and it is potentially very important.

Everyone has intuition to some degree but, like any other sensory characteristic, no two people experience it in exactly the same way. Some people may be very strongly tuned into those signals and understand something of the meaning of their own experiences. Others may have learned to ignore those signals and to try to tune them out.

The closer you get to your wedding day the harder it is to call it off. There is lots of social and financial pressure to continue on your path. So USE YOUR INTUITION EARLY AND OFTEN. Whenever you sense something is trying to emerge, pay particular attention to information a part of you may be trying to ignore. That's the information that might be critical to your future happiness.

He Seemed So Nice…

It is way too easy to be attracted to a man because he is new and different. You think he gives you what you want—which may be nothing more than an escape from a difficult situation. You may want to hurry up and make sure he doesn't change his mind. But unless you wait you may be seduced by surface traits that don't really match what fits into your life.

Part of taking time before you marry involves learning about your own patterns. Part involves being together long enough to learn how he changes under different circumstances.

Have you noticed that almost as soon as you get what you want you start to want something else? It's part of being human—he does it too.

You probably see it most clearly when choosing what you wear or the music you listen to. Your desires are influenced by what you see in stores and what your friends are wearing or listening to. Often what you thought you just had to have one month is completely abandoned a few months later. Certainly by the time a year passes you are ready for a change.

But sometimes you develop a favorite—maybe a purse or a jacket or a pair of earrings or a song—something that makes you feel good or happy every time you take it out and use it. You want to keep it even when it gets old and ratty. You didn't know that would happen; it took time for that preference to develop.

Sometimes giving yourself the time you need means giving yourself the time to learn about your own likes and dislikes—those things that stay relatively consistent over time instead of being influenced by the novelty of newness or by popularity. That also means learning the difference between what you are supposed to want and what really excites YOU—long term.

Anita puts it this way: "Be careful who you trust—time tells all. Don't be in a rush to move forward in the relationship—the longer you can wait, the more you will learn about the individual."

You Think This Time Will Be Better

Julie wishes she had "taken more time for myself before getting married again."

Patricia simply suggests, "Allow yourself time to absorb changes or ebb and flow of your relationship before making radical decisions. Give yourself some breathing room."

It doesn't matter if this is your first, your second or any subsequent marriage; you still need to take your time. Perhaps it's even more important if one of your marriages has failed.

Some women recognize making a mistake in one marriage and then make the opposite mistake in another marriage. Spouse #1 is so overbearing that wimpy, retiring spouse #2 seems like a perfect antidote. That works until you get so bored with spouse #2 that you are ready to light a fire under him to make something happen. Neither is a good choice.

Marianne, divorced, points out that taking your time is not the same as using your time to learn as much as you can about your prospective partner.

She suggests that you: "Know the potential spouse in as many different circumstances or experiences as possible before deciding on marriage. If you simply date without having adventures which require responses under pressure, you miss important information. Be sure you enter into activities you feel passionate about, cultural events, athletic events which you like to do regularly. Leave no stone unturned."

She did not know this until much later in her life. In describing the consequences of missing out on this important discovery, she wrote: "I did not do this as a thorough 'study' or opportunity to find out how he felt about the same things. We did not discuss how we felt about raising children; schooling, money matters, and what our goals in life were before marriage. That left space for disappointment later that we did not share similar values."

It's Okay to Wait

I waited. I met Jonathan just before my 19th birthday. Within a week after we met I was thinking in terms of "when we are married." He asked me to date him exclusively a month later and 3 months after that asked me to marry him. I said yes.

But I had an agreement with my parents to finish college before I married. I finished my remaining 2-½ years of school in just 1-½ years by going to summer school and carrying a heavy load. I kept my agreement but skipped my graduation ceremony because my wedding was taking place the next day in another city.

While we waited, we learned and grew and planned. We were ready to settle down but still had many things to learn before we could create a mature and loving marriage.

Liana Di Stefano of Australia did it differently. After a 12-year marriage, followed by a 12-year relationship with another man, followed by much exploration, she committed to a second marriage. She shares:

"Before I met my second husband, I arrived at a point that I was finally ready, at 45, to commit myself in marriage to someone for the rest of my life. I dated A LOT of men in a year. I became very clear in that process that I needed to meet my match—and I did. I was very clear that I would not be able to change this person so I had to be 100% ok with his character and traits/habits... and I am.

"In that year of dating I became very clear at reading the clues to behavior and what would eventually become a problem for us, and I became very good at honoring and trusting myself about whether to stay or go. I understood fully that the more I worked on my inner self, the better I would manifest my match. I learnt not to compromise on what I thought would work for me in relationship.

"Of course once I met my match, I knew/know that life is a matter of compromise at times so it's not about being unbending—but it was important that in the meeting phase I did not compromise on what I wanted and what I knew about myself about what would work or not for me.

"Marrying my husband gave me a sense of creating 'home' at a cellular level. I had spent so many years exploring relationships before I remarried, that there was nothing that I felt I didn't know before I remarried."

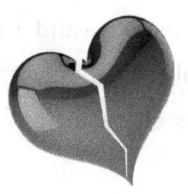

Chapter 4
Family Patterns are Important

"I wish I had known just how much family patterns could influence our marriage."

"What families have in common the world around is that they are the place where people learn who they are and how to be that way."

—Jean Illsley Clarke

Your Past Impacts Your Expectations

After 14 years of marriage, Rachel wishes she had known "that coming from different family backgrounds made such a big difference. His mother did not work. She hired people for tasks, but in my family we did everything ourselves."

Rachel didn't discover the problem until she asked her husband to help with the household chores. When he said, "Just hire someone," she was appalled. That was not her idea of how to use their limited resources. Besides, she took pride in her ability to do so many useful things by herself.

Over ten years later they still need to spend lots of time negotiating what tasks they each do and which ones they choose to have done by paid help.

As a child, you absorbed the background of your family without thinking about it. Since it was all you knew and experienced, you never questioned whether it was right, wrong or neutral—it was just the way things were. If you always slept in a bed, you quickly came to expect to sleep in a bed. On the other hand, if you always slept in a mat on the floor, or in a hammock slung between two trees, that's what you expected to continue to do. In other words, as a child, you expected whatever you were accustomed to. And, to a large extent, you still do.

It can be either an exciting adventure or a horrifying experience to learn that others do things very differently. Whether it is exciting or horrifying also depends on your family background. If change was welcomed as an opportunity for exploration, you are excited at the prospect of doing something new and different. But if change was judged and criticized in your family, you probably tend to resist it, even if the change might be for the better.

In any case, it's important to know that your family backgrounds *do* matter. If you don't know how much you are influenced by your early family experiences, you and your husband may both be shocked by how different your "right way" is from his "right way."

BEING MARRIED

Each Family Has Different Rules

Within those general backgrounds that depend largely on what continent you happened to be born on and the economic status of your family, each family also has its own set of rules. These rules can cover every aspect of family life.

- Who drives the car when the family goes out together?

- Who cooks?

- Who cleans up?

- Do you save and pay cash for a large purchase or do you use credit to pay for it?

- Do you pay off your credit cards monthly or carry a balance and make minimal payments?

- Do you attend a church or synagogue or mosque? How often?

- Are the children allowed to talk back to the adults?

- Do you go to baseball games or theater openings, or both, or neither?

- Do you wear your shoes inside the home or remove them?

- Do you eat dinner together? In the kitchen, in the dining room, or in front of the TV?

- Who uses computers and other electronic devices? When? Where?

- Do you watch TV together? How often? Who chooses the show?

- Do you rent or buy movies, vacation homes, tools, etc.?

- Who makes the choices and who follows along?

- Do you bathe in the morning or the evening? Every day or less frequently?

The list is endless, and you can be pretty sure your husband's family did things differently from yours. You can also be pretty sure each of you firmly believes that the way your family did it is the right way to do it. Of course, if you disagreed with the way your parents chose to do things, you may strongly believe that their way was wrong and a different way is correct.

It doesn't really matter who believes what. What *is* important here is to recognize that you each have a different set of unexamined beliefs about what is right. The more you can learn about these beliefs before you marry, the fewer unpleasant surprises you will encounter. That's why the premarital counseling offered by so many religious organizations can be helpful. It lets you explore and discuss some of the important differences before they can derail your relationship.

Joyce Asmus warns: "You must study his family and their style of communication, money-management, and conflict resolution. Their way will be his way, since that is the environment he grew up in. You cannot change that."

She adds, "If changes must be made for you to be compatible, first he has to WANT to change. Second, if changes are needed, a therapist should be enlisted to mediate them. This prevents one partner from dominating the exchange and/or the agreed-upon solutions."

I would add that most couples can learn the negotiation skills needed to resolve most differences. A good time to call in a counselor, therapist or other mediator is when you get stuck in the negotiation process.

New Situations Challenge Old Rules

Many couples live very happily together for a long time until they actually marry. Then, as soon as they are officially husband and wife, the family rules about what *married* people should do are activated. They are stunned by how much they argue with each other. Sadly, many divorce.

The problem is that the rules are hidden until they are activated and exposed. There is no way to change them ahead of time. Just be prepared to discuss them if they don't work for either you or your husband.

Being Married

Take Yvonne's hidden belief that all marriages are war zones: "I wish I knew that it could be better than my parents'. My parents fought constantly." She expected fights and got them until she learned that there were other options.

Amy wishes she had known "how different child-rearing ideas can cause strain during the early years with children." If they had recognized the reasons for those different ideas it might have been much easier to work out their differences.

Ron and Meredith did recognize how their old beliefs about how chores should be divided were interfering with their current happiness. One day Meredith looked up from cleaning the kitchen and saw Ron outside cutting the grass. She thought about how she hated being in the kitchen and wished she could be outside. Then she noticed how miserable he seemed to be; sweating and sneezing while he worked. She offered to trade chores. He accepted. They were both delighted with the change and bragged to their friends about how clever they were to make it, which is how I learned their story.

Different Family, Different Rules

If the rules you learned from your family work to enhance your relationship, you probably won't notice them and they won't matter. The problem comes when the rules you have absorbed actually interfere with being happy in your own marriage.

Cynthia, like most people who grow up in distressed families, did not know how her struggle to get along in that family impacted her marriage. She wishes "that I could have been aware of the unhealthy dynamics in my family (instead of repressing that knowledge for survival's sake) and had worked through those dynamics so that I could have entered marriage with less baggage."

Constance recognized that what she had learned from her mother's example unknowingly influenced her own behavior. She says: "I would have liked to understand that the patterns of relating to a man I learned from my mother were not all roses—to have seen more clearly her manipulation, coldness, unkindness and downright rebellion and disrespect towards my dad, instead of being snowed by the martyr façade she hid in."

It is very hard to see these patterns in yourself until real damage has been done to your marriage. One way to recognize that something is wrong is to listen to what you say to yourself and your closest friends about your relationship.

- If your words sound like a persecutor and you keep talking about what is wrong with him, especially in a mean or nasty way;

- If you talk about how hard you try to help him and rescue him from his problems but it never works;

- If you feel like a helpless victim and whine, blaming him for everything that isn't perfect;

Then it is time to change something. Persecutors, rescuers and victims have no place in a healthy relationship.

Both self-help groups like Al-Anon and professional counselors or therapists can help when you can't make the changes on your own. You'll save yourself a lot of distress if you seek help sooner rather than later.

Learn to Recognize His Family's Rules

Donna sums it all up by simply saying, "I wish I had noticed how he treated his mother."

When you think about it, doesn't how he treats his own mother really tell you a lot about a man? Especially if you start to play detective.

- If he treats his mother courteously, he will probably expect your children to treat you courteously.

- If he is overly concerned with pleasing her, it may mean that it will be difficult for him to act independently of her, and he may have a hard time switching his loyalty to you.

- If he is rude and defensive around his mother, it may mean that he does not yet feel independent and needs to push her away in order to feel like an adult. (It doesn't matter how old he is.) Or it may mean that he believes that women are inferior to men and not worthy of respectful treatment. It also may mean that he is imitating the way his father treats his mother. In that case, this is probably how he will treat you.

- If he respectfully disagrees with her but is willing to discuss their differences, it probably means that he has a mature and independent relationship with her and that he has definitely moved beyond his role as a kid in the family.

It would also be useful to observe how his mother treats him. He may expect you to treat him the same way. When you do, he will probably treat you the same way he treats her. She will also continue to treat him the same way after you are married, and you will need to decide whether or not that may cause problems for you.

Nikki is appalled when her mother-in-law treats her 32-year-old husband, who has a responsible job, as if he were a high-school student. It is very hard for her to have a good relationship with his mother because of her feelings.

Amy says: "I wish I had known more about his family and their dynamics. It took many years of getting to know them in all their dysfunction before I truly understood many things about my husband."

Every family has its own style and its own problems. Having the opportunity to get to know your husband's family before you say "I do" will help you make plans about how to cope with them—or may lead you to want additional talks with your fiancé about his family before your marriage.

Being Married

Expectations about Following Rules Cause Problems

Several women had a lot to say about this point, but Patricia put it most succinctly: "Choose your in-laws very carefully. They are a big part of the package, even if they don't live in the same state."

No matter where they live, there are remnants of them living in your husband, just as remnants of your parents reside in every fiber of your being. You can hear their voices any time you stop and listen, and when you are stressed, those words tend to come out of your mouth when they will do the most damage.

A theory for understanding yourself and others, Transactional Analysis (TA), calls this internal/external system your Parent Ego State. When I learned this simple, powerful system over 40 years ago, it changed my life. It is still one of the best tools I know of for helping people manage the sticky places in their lives and relationships.

You each create your Parent Ego State based on your early life experiences. You can consciously update this ego state based on your thoughtful evaluation of your life experiences. You can also choose to not follow the rules even when you feel a pull to do so. I have listed some useful TA materials in the Bibliography.

The problems come when you then must find a way to make peace with the living source of those rules: your respective families. And as circumstances change you will be exposed to information that may distress you.

Jeanette thought she had made a wonderful choice until her in-laws volunteered to keep her 18-month-old toddler son in their home overnight. Then she started observing the physical hazards in the home in which her husband had grown up. When she asked her husband's parents to make some simple adjustments they refused; saying what had worked for their children would work fine for their grandchildren.

Fortunately her husband Mike backed her up and supported her through her emotional turmoil until they reached a compromise.

Bailey sums it up: "The thing that people do not realize and they THINK they can ignore is, Yes, you do marry into the other's family. And I believe that if you cannot stand the family it is nearly impossible to make a marriage work. There is just too much interaction when you start adding kids."

On the other hand, if you grew up in a difficult situation yourself, your in-laws can be a wonderful support system. Paula, who later divorced her husband, admits, "I loved his family, not him."

A delightful resource for managing a challenging relationship is *The Mother-In-Law Rules* by Sally Shields.

Codependency is a Cultural Expectation

Codependency is a mutual agreement that the needs of one partner in a relationship are more important than the needs of the other partner.

In general it means that one partner, historically the woman, is expected to sacrifice her own needs and wants in service to the needs and wants of her husband and children. The strange thing is that in a codependent marriage, the other person does not even notice these sacrifices. In fact, each of you may think you are the only one making sacrifices.

Traditional mid-20th-century marriages are based on codependency, on the mutual understanding that one partner's needs, wants and feelings are more important than the other's. This often means that one partner exploits and the other tacitly agrees to be exploited in service to the marriage.

In the 21st century, however, many couples want to do things differently. Problems show up when one partner has absorbed the expectations of codependency and tries to impose them on a partner with different ideas.

Judy says, "I wish I had understood how dangerous unspoken, unmet and unfulfilled expectations can be to a relationship."

Constance describes what happens when a couple gets stuck in this pattern: "It would have been better if I knew ahead of time that the pattern I'd grown up in, which I knew was dys-functional, was actually codependency. I wish I had known that this disease can manifest as the aggressive and overbearing behavior I experienced from my husband as well as my passive, learned-helplessness forms of control. These are two sides of the same coin—both are equally unhealthy and weak patterns of relating."

My husband once wanted to leave me for another woman because I tried so hard to please him that I became boring. This was a definite symptom of a codependency pattern. Some variation of this pattern is the hidden reason most of the couples I see in my practice seek counseling.

Changing is Challenging

When codependency is present it usually permeates every aspect of your marriage. It affects how you communicate, how you play, how you raise children, and how you manage household tasks, money, special occasions, and everything else. Going back to Transactional Analysis theory will help you understand why.

TA teaches that along with your Parent Ego State you also have other personality systems. These are known as your Child Ego State, where your feelings and impulses reside, and your Adult Ego State, where you process information with logic. (To make it easier to talk and write about these ego states, they are often referred to as simply the Parent, the Adult, and the Child.) In addition to its job of observing, analyzing and predicting outside events, an important function of the Adult Ego State is internal: to observe and mediate between your Parent's rule-based system and your Child's emotion-based system.

Your ego states interact with your husband's ego states. When you both use all your ego states you can discuss rules (both Parent Ego States), share emotional and physical intimacy (both Child Ego States) and solve problems together (both Adult Ego States.) You can also ask for, offer and receive nurturing from each other.

Being Married

But family rules that lead to codependent patterns teach you to automatically shut down some necessary and important parts of yourselves when you are together. The spouse who is more important at the moment gets to choose!

If he chooses emotion (Child) you must figure out what kind of care he needs and give it to him—maybe by providing an orderly home and good meals—using your Parent and Adult to manage the situation. Your Child and your needs don't count. Your resentment builds until it pops out in angry, controlling, or passive behavior.

Of course, if he chooses Parent and Adult roles, he takes control, while you take the Child position and do as you are told. He controls the money even if you earn part of it. He chooses what you both do with weekend time. You may like this for a while, but your resentment eventually shows up here too.

Whenever one of you happens to get to be the more important one, the other one gets resentful.

Codependent patterns were uncomfortable in the past, when the "breadwinner" was often assumed to be the more important partner. Now, however, when both partners work to create economic stability for the family, these patterns are even more damaging to individuals and to their relationships.

Changing these pervasive patterns means learning to never (well, almost never) give up using any part of yourself. This means that you must learn to discuss values, play, and solve problems together in any situation.

Recovering from Codependency

There is a big risk, in remaining in a codependent relationship: the damage to both of you increases over time and you may become bitter and resentful. Sooner or later the marriage is likely to end anyway. This would leave each of you free to enter another codependent relationship.

Being Married

You may believe the next relationship would *have* to be better, but it probably won't end up being better if you haven't learned how to use all of your ego states regardless of whether the other person is using all of his. Your codependent role will continue to attract men who want to play a complementary role.

You CAN do it. You can do it together, or you can do it separately. If you do it together, it can turn into a fantastic adventure that can lead to a strong, loving and mutually supportive long-term relationship. From the vantage point of over 50 years of married life, believe me, it's worth it!

It can be extremely difficult to change codependent patterns without outside help. Most "self-help" and "relationship-help" books and programs address aspects of how you can become a committed and independent participant in your own marriage. So do most therapists and marriage counselors.

My husband and I have devoted a large part of our professional lives to helping clients and other professionals address these issues. A very useful resource in this series is *Being Happy Together: What to Do to Keep Love Alive*, which gives you dozens of activities you can do together to practice growing your relationship.

Our best-selling book, *Recovery from Co-Dependency: It's Never Too Late to Reclaim Your Childhood*, also contains additional useful information, much more than I can include here.

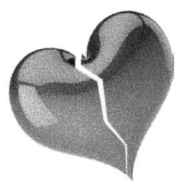

Chapter 5

You Don't Notice

Very Important Things

"*I wish I had noticed more about him ahead of time and that what he says doesn't always match what he does.*"

Surprising Reasons for Choices

This twice-married 50ish contributor did not leave her name, but her message is critical. She wishes she had known "that I wasn't making a clear choice of partner because of my upbringing." Her experience is almost universal.

As human beings, we seem to be hard-wired to spend our lives trying to complete the process of growing up. No parent is perfect and no parent (or parents) can possibly give any child everything she needs to become a mature and independent adult. This means that at some point we need to become fully responsible for parenting ourselves.

Many of us resist doing so because we don't want the responsibility, and maybe we're even afraid we aren't competent to look after ourselves, at least in some areas of our lives. If you haven't become a good parent to yourself by the time you marry, on an unconscious level you may expect your husband to take over the job.

Consciously you may create a list of characteristics for the man you are seeking. Just look at any dating site to see the lists. They include age, interests, ethnicity, education, location, physical characteristics, etc. But if "the chemistry is right," you may throw away your list and just fall in love.

That means you're excited because a part of you recognizes in your potential mate the very characteristics you have been trying to avoid in a partner. You are not consciously aware of this; instead, you think you're excited because you and he are so compatible: "We fit together perfectly." Unfortunately you may fit together in an unhealthy codependent way, but it feels right because it's what you were used to in your original family.

"I wish I had known that we are attracted to people who often have the same unhealthy traits and patterns as our parents," remarked Morgan.

Chemistry often means you have found someone who seems enough like your parents that you hope he can give you what they failed to give. It feels as if being with him will make you complete, as if he will fill in the aching holes you have suffered from all your life. It seldom works that way. You choose someone who is so much like one or both of your parents that he has the same inability to give you what you long for. Unless… something happens to help you both become aware of the situation.

JoAnn shares, "I wish I had known that I was marrying a man almost identical to my dad. I don't like my dad—he is not a nice man. He puts on a good show in front of other people, but he's very selfish, manipulative and controlling. Sadly, that was normal for me, and I attracted the same kind of man. It didn't work."

Sometimes when couples seek counseling, they each find that although it can be very challenging to give what their partner longs for, it's also extremely rewarding. In learning how to supply what the other person wants, they may discover exactly what they need for themselves and find out how to get it. Fulfilling each other's emotional needs and wants can lead to spectacularly good relationships.

Harville Hendrix describes this process in his bestselling book, *Getting the Love You Want*.

Looking Good Doesn't Last

Being Married

Susan, who at 64 is enjoying her fourth marriage, wishes she had known that "most people hide some of their more irritating habits/traits until after marriage."

Think back to those dating sites. When people describe themselves they never seem to say anything about being a slob; squeezing the toothpaste tube from the middle; being self-centered, controlling or critical; hating parties or dogs, etc. They list only their desirable characteristics.

During courtship, you try your best to please each other. You may not even notice each other's negative traits at first, when you're falling in love. You both want the relationship to work, so even if negative behaviors show up, you do your best to ignore them or make excuses for them.

An anonymous contributor says: "When you are treated like a princess until you marry someone who has progressive ideas, it comes as something of a shock to learn about his expectations of what meals should be and of how to handle finances, relationships with friends of the opposite gender, in-laws, etc."

Unconscious Choices Reflect Unresolved Issues

Parents usually do the best they can to give their children what the children need—but you can't give what you don't have yourself.

- If your mom was not allowed to say no when she was a child, and has not had another opportunity to learn to set limits, she can't help you learn about how to say no and set appropriate boundaries.

- If your own childhood exuberance was squashed, you tend to squash similar exuberance in your children.

- If you always saw your mom being obedient to your dad, you may learn that you are not supposed to be independent either.

But you do need to be able to set appropriate boundaries, act exuberant sometimes, and learn to be independent.

Being Married

Because you think you can't do those things yourself, you may be attracted to someone who can. He may be just like your dad—the very dad your mom chose because he could do those things and she couldn't.

Catherine wishes she had known "that I would likely choose a partner who would repeat my unhealed childhood wounds and that I would unwittingly help to recreate this problem." And Juanita wishes she had known her "subconscious reasons for choosing this type of husband."

There is no set formula for which of your parents' characteristics you will choose to look for in a partner, and it is not easy to sort this out. Nevertheless, you can avoid what happened to Catherine and Juanita. The more you know about yourself and your family and the more you try to fill the gaps by deliberately doing things that challenge you, the less vulnerable you will be to making unconscious and limiting choices.

Conscious and Unconscious Agreements

You make conscious agreements when you take your wedding vows. You have a pretty good idea of what you're agreeing to, although your husband may have a somewhat different interpretation of what those words mean.

The unconscious agreements are about doing what you each learned from observing your own families when you were children. Since your families were different, you may be unconsciously agreeing to very different things.

You may be agreeing to share your deepest thoughts and feelings with him, while he may be agreeing to grunt occasionally while you're speaking. You may be agreeing to cook food he likes, to be actively involved in making choices for the family, and to keep track of all social engagements. He may be agreeing to do all the maintenance on the cars, to be the main wage-earner, and to teach your children sports skills.

Meanwhile, he may think you're agreeing to follow his rules and defer to his decisions. You may think he is agreeing to always treat you like a queen.

Being Married

You both may secretly agree that he will protect you from needing to do things that scare you, like negotiating with the landlord to replace the appliances. In exchange, you may be agreeing to always treat him as if he were a glowing example of powerful masculinity.

On a deeper level you are setting up your own codependency agreements. It's like setting the automatic cruise control. You are making agreements that specify the areas in which his needs and feelings will be the most important and under what circumstances yours will count more. For example, you might agree that his needs count most under ordinary circumstances and yours count most only when you are sick or exhausted.

You may be agreeing to always put his needs first, and he may be agreeing that it's appropriate for you to do this.

You may be agreeing that he will take center stage with family and friends and you will stay in the background. Or it could be the other way around, with you in front while he stands behind you and supports you. One of you may be agreeing to be responsible for preparing meals for the family. Traditionally it would be you, but that is not always the case.

None of these agreements are inherently wrong. The problem is that you're not aware of having made them. If you inadvertently break them, your spouse will be confused and/or angry, and you won't know why. Likewise, you'll be confused and/or angry when he doesn't keep the agreements he didn't know he made, and your reaction may be very puzzling to him.

Hidden Expectations Cause Problems

You'll probably get confused the first time your expectation isn't met. You'll find yourself saying things like:

"How could you invite your brother to stay with us without consulting with me first?"

Response: "But it's my house."

Being Married

"Why didn't you tell me you would be delayed?! I expected you hours ago!"

Response: "I shouldn't have to."

Why don't you do some of the cooking?

Honest response: "I thought it was your job. My dad never did it."

Other common responses: "I thought you liked to cook" or "I don't know how."

Janet summarized this experience by saying, "I wish I had known it was all about him."

Rachel, who is still married to her husband, says a bit more generously, "I wish I had known that he was much more traditional than I thought and expected me to do all the cooking and cleaning." She thought he believed in shared responsibility, but his parents had a traditional marriage. The fact that his mother did not work outside the home and that Rachel had a full-time job didn't seem to make any difference to him.

When these disagreements show up you have choices.

- You can whine and complain about things not being what you expected them to be.

- You can give in and suffer silently until you can't stand it anymore.

- You can use force or manipulation to get him to do it your way.

- You can leave the marriage.

- You can learn to negotiate about how you want your marriage to be.

Negotiating an agreement may be like resetting the cruise control to a new speed: you may find that you can't set it once and for all. The setting goes away each time you restart the car, and you need to remember to reset it. Recalling this analogy may help you remember that matter-of-fact reminders work better then angry accusations when either of you forgets your new agreements.

BEING MARRIED

Notice Clues about Hidden Information

This is one of the best reasons for taking your time before actually committing to marriage. But during that time you do have to pay attention to what you see, hear and feel about his behavior instead of ignoring your own discomfort. If you catch yourself automatically excusing something he says or does, consider that a warning signal to pay closer attention.

Sandra was dissatisfied with her husband's ability to be close to her after they married. She wishes she had noticed "my hubby's missing capacity for intimacy in other relationships."

Barbara did notice her husband's behavior but didn't think it was particularly important. She wishes she had known "that people tend to treat their spouses like they treat pets and wait staff. Mine did not like any animal and always talked down to wait staff. He came to treat me the same way."

Janet learned to be watchful about an annoying behavior when she chose husband number two because the first time around she wished she "had noticed whether he reflects on his own behavior and makes appropriate changes." Her second husband does notice when his behavior causes her distress or doesn't get the results he wants, and he then adjusts it accordingly. He learns from experience and seldom repeats his mistakes.

One way to know what to attend to is to notice your own gut feelings or intuition. When you feel uncomfortable about something, don't dismiss it. Ask yourself why, and take time to track down and investigate the source of your discomfort.

The more you learn, the fewer surprises you will have to contend with. Even careful observation won't prevent all of those surprises, though. Remember, some of the programming about how to behave in a marriage does not activate until the marriage has taken place—or even a few years later, when you start having children.

You must always be prepared to notice when you need to correct your course.

Being Married

Those Not-So-Fatal Attractions

"The traits that attracted you in the first place may drive you crazy later because you don't recognize those traits in yourself."

Barbara wishes she had known "that the traits that attract a person often become the traits that irritate the most."

That's because you had to suppress the traits that weren't approved of in your own family when you were a child. For example, if exuberance wasn't allowed, you are naturally curious about what it's like to experience exuberant, energetic behavior, so you may be fascinated with someone you meet who is free to express his exuberance. He becomes very attractive to you.

At the same time, you have learned the values of your own family, and although his high energy fascinates you, a part of you disapproves of it just as your parents did. Another part of you is a little afraid that if you express your own energy you will be punished in some way.

Here's another example: When you grow up in a family where females are not supposed to show anger, two different things may happen. First, when you are a child you may be punished for showing anger or simply told that you are not really angry. (For example, "You're just tired," or "You're just upset.") Second, when angry feelings naturally arise, you quickly put them out of your awareness. If someone asks you if you're angry, you probably deny it because you don't even recognize it in yourself.

So even though you've learned that anger is bad and you think you're not an angry person, angry people are sort of interesting. They may remind you of your father who was allowed to be angry. You find an angry guy who fascinates you and marry him. A few years later his anger at red lights and bad drivers becomes very annoying.

There's also another side to your attraction. Feeling anger is part of being human. Even though you have learned never to acknowledge them, you sometimes do have

Being Married

angry feelings that need expression or release. In a strange and paradoxical way, your angry husband does this for you. (It's a dirty job, but someone has to do it!) When he shows the anger you don't allow yourself to express, you can experience this vicariously and feel a sense of relief, even if you are consciously deploring his behavior.

You also never learned that anger is really energy that's meant for solving problems. And of course, with anger being forbidden, you never got any practice in using that energy productively.

I believe that finding my own anger saved my marriage over 50 years ago. When my husband told me he wanted to leave me for another woman, I was furious. My anger exploded, and I think that energy convinced him that I really cared about him. I don't recommend doing it the way I did. My excuse is that my hormones made me do it—after all, I was pregnant at the time.

Taking back your own anger by learning safe and appropriate ways to express it will make you much less vulnerable to being upset by your husband's anger.

Of course, the same thing is true of any other trait you think belongs to your husband and not to you. If you were attracted by his boldness because you are timid, you need to learn to be bold also. If you were attracted by his stability because you felt it would balance your flightiness—and are now bored silly because he's a stick-in-the-mud—you need to learn to be responsible also.

After all, each of these traits is part of being a complete, effective human being. When you claim your own share of each trait, then your husband's behavior will no longer have the power to drive you crazy.

You Can't Make Him Change

Suzanne puts it this way: "I wish I had known how important it is to marry someone you're completely happy with, and who is completely happy with you. Neither of you are likely to change; that should not be an expectation."

Being Married

People can change. My job is to help people through their change processes, and my clients do change. Remember this old joke? "How many people does it take to change a light bulb?" "Only one, but the light bulb has to *want* to change." This may not be true of light bulbs, but it is true of people: individuals change only because they want to change, for reasons of their own. The reason is never that someone else thinks it would be a good idea for them to change.

That's why "chasing your spouse around the house with a self-help book" never works. I love this image from John Bradshaw, author of many self-help books. Actually, however, your spouse just might look at the book if you leave it sitting unobtrusively in the bathroom. In this series, *Relationship Tips for Life Partners*, is especially good for this purpose.

Change takes time and attention, and many people would rather leave a relationship than engage in making changes. If you would prefer to remain in your relationship but realize you are not living the life you desire and deserve, you may be motivated to learn new ways of being together. When you do, get help. It's available from many sources: books, courses, seminars, retreats, support groups, and helping professionals.

You need outside help so that you don't spend extra time and energy reinventing the wheel. Many people have been where you are now and know what it takes to create a successful marriage.

If your husband isn't ready to make changes, you can take the first steps yourself. As you change how you relate with your husband, he may be reassured that it's safe to move forward and make his own changes.

It may help to remember that change and growth are a necessary part of being alive and that change is always occurring.

Being Married

Learning Together Works

Juanita and JoAnn did make changes and were happy with the results.

Juanita wishes she had known "I could shift to what I really wanted and 'deserved' rather than repeating my parents' incompatibility."

JoAnn shares: "I've learned a lot about myself - who I am, what's important to me, and that I am important, loveable, deserve to be treated well, respected and cherished by myself first, others after! Wow, what a lesson! Too bad I had to do it the hard way!"

The challenging things you may need to do in order to change include learning to listen carefully to your husband and understand what he means by his words. This may sound easy, but it isn't. It means clarifying with him what you think you've heard when all you want to do is defend yourself. It's worth it, though. Especially when your husband learns the same lessons you do.

I often find that couples really want the same thing but disagree about how to achieve their goals. Once they listen to each other long enough to understand this, arguments become problem-solving sessions.

You may also learn that you have hurt your spouse as well as being hurt by him. This can be an opportunity for both of you to heal.

Learning to give your spouse what he wants, instead of what you think he should have, may be difficult. But it may not be as difficult as learning to risk asking for what you want and then finding out that you don't necessarily get it even when you do ask. And then continuing to ask and negotiate anyway, because you're worth it.

You may need to learn to stand up for yourself and negotiate. You may even need to learn to back down after attempts to negotiate because you've decided it makes sense to do so, and because you know you're moving on instead of giving in.

Remember, help makes it easier to change. Meet these challenges by getting help from knowledgeable people, reliable books, support groups, and courses that are listed in the resource section. You'll find the rewards are well worth your efforts.

Chapter 6
You Need to Discuss Your Values

"I wish we had talked about values before we got married, instead of fighting about them after we were married."

Your Mask Won't Keep You Safe

When beginning a relationship, it's natural for potential partners to show only those things they think will make them attractive to the other person.

Being Married

Since no one is someone without a disguise,
And the truths of the parlor, in the bedroom are lies,

And my everyday self is a shoddy disgrace,
I'll put on this mask to show you my face.

—Maurice English 1909—1983

Dating is especially tough when you're trying to find the right life partner. You each want to be the right person, but you have to feel your way along.

You don't put on an arbitrary mask; you put on the mask that you think will be the most attractive to your new potential partner. Of course, you don't know for sure what that will be. You may have searched magazines and self-help books for information about what makes women attractive. Or you may have learned by trial and error in your dating career or in other relationships.

It's quite likely that the man you are with is doing exactly the same thing.

Like Ruth, age 75, who's been married three times, you may think it makes you attractive to always defer to a man. Now Ruth says, "I wish I had known that it wasn't my job to pretend that the man was always right."

You each put up a façade, the one you think will do the best job of both protecting the parts of you that you think may make you unattractive and showing what you think your potential partner wants to see. Then you respond to the façade that you see in front of you, and then you wonder why you don't really know each other.

What You Talk about Matters

You don't get to test your communication skills if you talk only about fun and easy things.

You get to know each other by talking for hours. You share so many things that you think you really know each other well. You certainly don't challenge each other by disagreeing with anything, even if you're a little uncomfortable about it. You tell yourself there will be plenty of time for that later.

You tend to avoid sticky subjects because you're afraid of messing things up. You talk about your successes but not your failures or your challenges. If you have children, you may talk about the fun things you do with them, but you probably won't talk about your frustration with disciplining them.

Sometimes you start a relationship based around problems you're experiencing in a different relationship. You share a little bit with someone you know casually, and he responds with sympathy for your plight. He actually listens to you and seems to appreciate you. Then he tells you about his struggles in his current relationship, and you listen and appreciate his sensitivity. You base your new relationship on the shared experience of being someone else's victim, and on rescuing each other from victimization.

Or perhaps you just listen and affirm everything he says. And you ask questions to get him to say more because you heard that being a good listener is the best way to attract a man. And it does attract him. It convinces him that any future relationship will revolve around him. By the time you start to wonder when it will be *your* turn to be heard and affirmed, it's too late: he isn't likely to want to give up his place at the center of your universe.

Ask—Never Assume

When you affirm each other without ever asking hard questions, you both begin to think you agree about everything. This illusion is enhanced by the human tendency to assume that others see the world in exactly the same way you do.

Marianne wishes she had spent more time learning her fiancé's thoughts and opinions about important things. She shares what is true for many couples: "Before we married we did not discuss how we felt about raising children, schooling, money matters, and what our goals in life were." Sara, a married woman wishes she and her husband had known "each other's personal goals for education and career." Michelle wishes she "had asked the 'what if' questions." During courtship, couples often fail to discuss family traditions and potential life transitions, assuming these things either will be no problem or will be worked out easily as they go along.

Again and again I have seen assumptions like these cause problems for my clients who believe:

- That your spouse will follow you to whatever city your company sends you.

- That you'll celebrate holidays exactly the way your parents did.

- That you'll save money for large purchases.

- That you'll run your credit up to the limit.

- That your spouse wants children.

- That you intend to advance in your position.

- That you both want the same kinds of vacations (luxurious, driving, camping, beach, mountains,

- active, restful, visiting relatives, traveling abroad, etc.)
- That you'll drop out of school—or stay in school.
- That your parents will babysit—or that they won't.

The possibilities for confusion and disappointment are endless.

One way to avoid this common situation is through premarital counseling or premarital courses that identify potential areas of conflict and encourage couples to talk about these issues before they get married. It's well worth taking the time to do so.

Some Differences Really Do Matter

Linda, who's been married for 30 years, wishes she had known "that we need to have similar values." Ann wishes she had known "that people do change over time. Be sure you have the same core values and agree on the big things."

If something is important to you, you may assume that it's equally important to your husband. Before you marry, it can be easy to ignore behavior that suggests he may not share your values. When you do notice that kind of behavior, you may either create excuses for it or tell yourself it doesn't really matter. Worse yet, you may assume that he will change once you are married. (There's another of those dangerous assumptions!)

You may be certain that he'll keep his promise to quit smoking, or drink less, or get a better job. It doesn't occur to you that if all his friends smoke, or if he always keeps a couple of six-packs in the refrigerator, or if he's been in the same dead-end job for several years, it may be very hard for him to keep his promise.

What he's doing now can be a pretty good indication of what he will do after you're married. If he's a workaholic who constantly checks his e-mail and takes phone calls and responds to text messages even when you're together at an elegant restaurant, it would be pretty unrealistic to expect him to devote his complete attention to you after you're married,

Unfortunately, when you're madly in love, it's easy to ignore what may be obvious to your friends and family. When your best friend points out something questionable about your fiancé's behavior, you could brush off her comments by telling yourself she's just jealous of your happiness and resentful of his taking your time and attention away from her. Even if she actually is a bit jealous, that doesn't mean her observations would be invalid. After all, she knows you well and cares about you, as do your other friends and family members. If any of these people raise red flags, it's time to wake up and pay attention.

It's hard to make a marriage work when you and your husband disagree about what's really important. It's worth it to take the time to learn about each other's values before you say, "I do."

Being Married

Defensiveness is Dangerous

When there is disagreement, it's easy to take this personally and feel unloved. You say to yourself, "If you really loved me, you would not only know what I want, you would want to give it to me." After saying this to yourself a few times, you might find yourself saying it out loud.

Sometimes you may disagree about something as simple as how things should work when you share a bathroom. You may find yourself saying something like this: "If you really loved me, you'd pick up after yourself." Then the third time, or maybe the fifth time he leaves his towel on the floor, you up the ante and complain: "I'm tired of always being treated like the maid!" Or "I'm not your mother!" If he continues failing to comply with your wishes, you might even start attacking his character or calling him names: "You are so inconsiderate!" "You're such a slob."

Then the fight is on, and it's not even about how to agree on what to do about the bathroom. You try to hurt each other because you each feel so hurt yourselves. You expect to be loved unconditionally, and suddenly you each discover that you are supposed to meet very definite conditions that may seem absurd to you. And you don't even know how to talk about it.

You bring in past history about how you felt slighted when he looked admiringly at another woman. (Now, what does that have to do with who hangs up the towels?) Then he talks about your recent conversation with your old boyfriend, and you defend yourself, saying it was about his sister who used to be your friend. He goes out and slams the door, and you call your best girlfriend and cry.

A few hours later he comes home and acts as if nothing ever happened. You wonder what to do, but that seems like a good solution, so you act the same way.

About the tenth time you go through this cycle you wonder if you're going to have to get a divorce.

Being Married

Admitting Your Vulnerability Lets You Connect

This isn't what you expected, and it feels awful.

It wouldn't have happened if you had had the skills to talk about what's really important to you. The fewer skills you have, the more energy you may spend feeling like a victim and trying to defend yourself by proving that your partner is wrong. When you do that, he feels like the victim and fights back.

When that doesn't work, either or both of you may promise to do better and then not keep your promises. You probably don't keep them because you promised to do something you don't want to do at all, or something you *can't* do because you lack the skill or the resources. The promises work for awhile, but then the fighting starts again because of the broken promises.

Then you may try to do everything right. Before long, however, you get frustrated because it feels like you're walking on eggshells and you still haven't solved the basic problems.

It feels like an endless circle, going nowhere. There is a way out, though. You can show your vulnerability. You start by admitting that you feel afraid and helpless and that you don't want to continue to hurt your partner. You can shift the focus away from how miserable you are and take the step of trying to understand what your partner really wants. If you learned active listening skills at work, now is the time to bring them home, to make certain you understand what your partner is telling you.

This is very challenging, and shifting the focus to your partner may be more than you can manage on your own. Or it may be that the focus is already on your partner. If that's the case, it can be extremely difficult to get your partner to respond to you in a positive way. You need help, and it's important to get it before things get any worse.

With any luck, one of you will make an appointment with a marriage counselor (or other helping professional) who can help you listen to each other and start to have the important conversations you should have had before you were married.

Nobody Wins a Power Struggle

If you don't get help and you keep trying to change each other, you can get locked into a power struggle that lasts for years. Each of you thinks that if only you could take control of the situation, you could fix it.

Several years after her divorce, Debra says, "I wish I had known that I took up all the space and so didn't learn very much about my potential spouse." She had spent much of their marriage trying to help him become more ambitious and successful. He rewarded her by making promises and not keeping them. She didn't notice that what she wanted him to do had very little to do with what he wanted to do. Only by ending the marriage was she able to disengage from the power struggle.

The power struggle is really about the struggle we each have with our own parents to prove, as little kids sometimes say, "You're not the boss of me!" The way out of the power struggle is to step back and admit the truth: you are *not* the boss of your spouse. You are two independent people who have decided to make a life together. You can't force each other to do anything. It's the simple truth.

What you can do is identify what you want, discover what your husband wants, and learn to talk about your reasons for those desires. Then you can talk about your resources and plan the most effective way for you each to get as many important things as you possibly can. This process may not sound very dramatic, but it's an important step toward developing a marriage that supports you both.

A Disagreement Isn't a Disaster

In her second marriage, Lisa discovered this: "When you have kids, you need to let your husband be the co-CEO and make child-rearing decisions cooperatively. You need to be on the same page."

Being Married

Disagreeing doesn't mean your husband is disloyal; it just means his ideas are different from yours because his background is different from yours. No matter how similar your families and your life experiences may seem, there are always differences. You can resolve these by learning to disagree without being disagreeable.

You each survived, and even thrived, doing things the way your original families did them.

- In one family, children had regular bedtimes. In the other, bedtimes were flexible.

- In one family, the children's needs came first. In the other, the children needed to adapt to their parents' work schedules.

- In one family, children did regular chores. In the other, homework came before everything else and was a way to get excused from chores.

- One family went to church every Sunday. The other family went only at Christmas and Easter.

- One family opened gifts on Christmas Eve. The other family waited until Christmas morning.

- In one family, children got generous allowances. In the other family, children had to earn their spending money.

The list goes on and on. None of those practices are wrong, and each one has its own impact on what children learn about the world. Instead of arguing about which one is right, it works much better to discuss what you want your children to learn from each experience.

Even after discussion, you may still disagree. If so, one of you may decide to give in because the other has stronger feelings about that particular issue. You can work things out as long as you believe that both you and your spouse ultimately have similar goals for your children.

The same strategy works in other areas of your marriage.

Communicating is Critical

When I ask a new couple why they have come for counseling, the most common answer I get is: "We just don't communicate."

Combining the responses I've received from several women into one response, what these women wish they had known is "how to communicate effectively through tough times, in emotionally charged situations."

What passes for communication in many marriages looks like this: One person is busy doing some task, watching TV or checking text messages, while the other one is talking. The busy one nods occasionally or grunts every so often. Later, when the subject comes up again, the one who was speaking says, "But I told you all about it. Don't you remember?"

"Not communicating" means a variety of different things:

- That anything you say seems to be misunderstood, and the conversation turns into an argument.

- That you keep trying to explain how you feel and what you want, and your partner simply doesn't understand what you mean.

- That you just don't understand what your partner is talking about.

- That you disagree with what your partner is saying and don't know how to tell him without upsetting him.

- That anything your partner says feels like he's attacking you, and either you spend all your time defending yourself or you feel helpless and crumble instead of explaining your own point of view.

"Not communicating" usually includes being so busy thinking about what you want to say, or about something else entirely, that you really don't listen to your partner's words, let alone to the meaning behind the words.

There are dozens of resources to help you and your husband learn to communicate. One of my favorites is the

Being Married

Being Happy Together book, which has 125 different activities you can complete in less than an hour a week. It's described in the resource section.

In any case, the first step to effective communication is your intention to not only *give* information but to *exchange* information. You might be surprised at how much impact you can have on a difficult situation by simply listening carefully and then demonstrating that you have understood what you've heard.

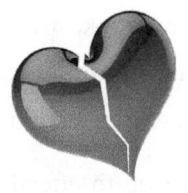

Chapter 7
Physical Issues Take Attention and Communication

"I wish I'd known just how important that physical stuff really is."

Physical Attraction: Necessary But Not Sufficient

Especially when you are of childbearing age, physical attraction may be the main reason your relationship began. This is explained by the "selfish gene" theory: your

Being Married

genes are trying to reproduce themselves, whether you like it or not. That makes you particularly vulnerable to letting your hormones choose your partner.

This vulnerability is one reason I suggest that my clients not have sexual relationships with anybody with whom they would not like to raise a child. It's another good reason to avoid using sex as a way of getting to know somebody. Physical attraction often gets in the way of learning about each other. Having good sex together is only one criterion for creating a loving and lasting relationship.

It is, however, a necessary criterion. An anonymous fiftyish married responder wrote: "I wish I had known how important it is that you not deny the need to be physically attracted to your future spouse."

Two good friends, both single and searching, would be a perfect match for each other in every way except, unfortunately, sexually. She reported, "We decided to give it a try, but it was like kissing my brother."

On the other hand, if you are marrying young to escape a difficult family situation, you may not even be prepared for a sexual relationship. Janelle was so appalled by her initial sexual encounter that all she could do was wander the streets, trying to think of a way to escape her new marriage. Her wish was "that I had been more experienced in sex before getting married."

Physical Intimacy—Multiple Meanings

People may express and feel intimacy in many different ways. Loving touch, with or without intercourse, is often one of those ways. Some individuals, however, experience real intimacy only through sexual contact.

An anonymous woman wrote, "I wish I had known that sex was so important to my husband." She is a lot like Grace who, with her husband, was in one of our couples' workshops many years ago. When Grace mentioned to her husband that she really was not much interested in continuing to have intercourse, he was horrified! Then she was shocked when he told the workshop participants that he needed a sexual act as proof that he was really loved.

Many couples complain that the passionate sex they enjoyed in the early part of their relationship was not sustained. If the level of passion in a relationship declines, some individuals believe this means they are falling out of love. They therefore end the relationship and seek renewed **passion with a new and exciting partner. The** belief that decreased passion means decreased love can lead to a series of short, unsatisfying relationships.

For most couples, however, nature takes its course: once the "selfish genes" are satisfied, the sexual relationship assumes different forms and intensities as the marriage develops. Information about cycles of relationship development is available in the *Being Happy Together* book and in a complimentary MP3 recording that's available when you "like" the "99 Things Women Wish They Knew before Saying I Do" page on Facebook.

You Each Must Define Enough

A wonderful scene in the old Woody Allen movie, Annie Hall, shows a split screen in which each member of a couple is talking to a different therapist. His therapist asks him, "How often do you have sex?" He replies, "Hardly ever! Only two or three times a week." Her therapist asks her the same question. She replies, "All the time! At least two or three times a week!"

Karen wishes she had known "how often he would want to have sex."

People differ greatly in their desire for sexual contact. For some, it provides physical relief; for others, it affirms emotional connection. As a general rule, more women than men want to have emotional contact before they move into sexual contact. Many men would prefer just sexual contact, with minimal emotional interaction.

Most couples learn to accommodate to each other's rhythms, especially when they can speak directly to each other about what they need. When they don't have direct conversations, they often use physical issues, such as being tired or having a headache, as excuses for not accommodating one another.

Unfortunately, a man may believe that a marriage license entitles him to sexual relations anytime he wants them. It doesn't, and he isn't! If he persists in having relations with you after you have said no, you are being raped. You do not have to be accommodating just because you are married.

Counselor and author Linda Lee Landon emphasizes to her clients and her daughter that NO is a complete sentence.

If your husband doesn't understand this concept, get counseling or leave the marriage—or both—and the sooner the better!

Communicate about Sexual Problems

Debra, twice divorced, wishes she had known it was even possible "to deal with his early ejaculation issue without all the judgment and resentment. He tried to be a good lover, but that got in the way."

If you consider sexual problems as shameful, you keep them to yourself. You don't want anybody to know that you don't match the ideals of femininity or masculinity as they are portrayed in the media. You may even pretend to yourself, or to each other, that there are no sexual problems in your relationship. Even if you are able to acknowledge the problems, you certainly don't want to talk about them, so you try these damaging strategies.

If you have never experienced orgasm, or don't feel as if you are moving toward orgasm in a particular sexual encounter, you may simply pretend to have reached climax. You may do this so your lover can believe he has pleased you and has demonstrated his virility. On the other hand, you may simply want to end an unsatisfactory sexual experience and be allowed to go to sleep. Or you may pretend to have orgasms in order to hide your embarrassment at not responding adequately.

Being Married

Sometimes one of you will blame the other for an unsatisfactory sexual encounter. You may say he didn't shower and smells bad and turned you off. He may accuse you of deliberately being cold. You may avoid talking about what pleases you sexually because of shyness or because you tried to convey that information in the past and received an unsympathetic or accusatory response.

Every one of these attempts to avoid discussing sexual issues will serve to drive you farther apart.

Help is available in many forms. For example, there are medical websites where trained professionals have provided accurate answers to common sexual questions. But please be careful when attempting to access sexual information on the Internet. You will need to take precautions to avoid sites that may dispense misinformation or, as some pornographic sites do, may introduce malware or allow unauthorized access to information stored on your computer. You can avoid these hazards by entering "reputable medical websites" into a search engine and then searching only within those sites for articles containing sexual information.

You may also wish to consult a sex therapist who is specially trained and board certified to assist with sexual problems. Your gynecologist or primary care physician can provide a referral to a sex therapist, or you can find one yourself, perhaps through a local hospital, a friend, or the Internet.

Sleeping Problems Interfere with Intimacy

All of us are subject to a hierarchy of needs, and the most fundamental of those is survival. Sleep is a survival need. If you need sleep, that takes precedence over any need for physical contact or intimacy. On the one hand, this seems pretty simple: survival needs must be met first. On the other hand, as human beings, we can complicate almost anything.

Your natural rhythms may or may not match each other. Some people are at their best in the morning and others in the evening. Again, the problem stems from each of you believing that everyone else is, or should be, exactly like you. Ascribing evil intent to a simple mismatch in biological rhythms or needs will definitely cause unnecessary problems.

You may have a mismatch in many areas around sleeping:

- One of you may need complete darkness, and the other may like to fall asleep with the TV on.

- One of you may toss and turn, while the other barely moves.

- One may be disturbed by the slightest noise, while the other can sleep through a thunderstorm.

- One of you may be able to sleep well only if the room is cool, while the other likes the room to be toasty-warm.

- One or both of you may snore and disturb each other.

- One of you may like to hit the snooze button several times before getting out of bed, while the other may deeply resent being awakened any sooner than necessary.

- One of you may like to cuddle, while the other may prefer not to be touched during sleep.

- Pregnancy, menopause, illness, work schedules, babies, and untold other things can also create sleep problems.

One of the worst sleeping experiences of my marriage happened when the dual controls of our electric blanket were accidentally switched. I spent the night shivering and turning up "my" control to get warm. My husband spent the night sweating and turning down "his" control trying to cool off. We were both miserable and couldn't figure out why until morning.

Blaming each other for sleep problems is pointless. If you and your husband can't be comfortable in the same sleeping situation, you could decide to do something a bit unconventional. As Emily learned, "Sleeping in the same bed isn't the cornerstone of marriage. If using two bedrooms works for you and you both sleep better... it's OK!"

What's most important is talking about sleep problems and searching for a solution together.

Health Issues Can Become Critically Important

An illness or an accident can completely disrupt your life and your marriage.

We seldom think about health issues until they begin to present problems. It's completely natural to imagine ourselves as invincible and to avoid thinking about the possibility of illness, injury, or disability. Nevertheless, sooner or later, physical or mental health issues are likely to affect our relationships. This is why many marriage vows include the phrase "in sickness and in health," warning us to be prepared to deal with any health challenges that may arise.

It's important to share any health information you do have, to help you make informed decisions about potential problems.

- Gretchen, a married woman, wishes she had known about "my husband's health history, as he has a genetic disease that was passed to one of our children."

- Although Jessica knew her fiancé was diabetic, she didn't realize all the implications of this. She says, "I wish I had known what it really meant to have diabetes. I didn't think it was a big deal because he seemed fine. He didn't talk about it much and never complained. I had no idea about everything he had to do and not do in order to stay healthy—and what could happen to him if he didn't. I'm sorry now that I didn't know what it would take for both of us to cope with his disease."

Being Married

- Elizabeth was infuriated when she developed genital herpes: "He hadn't had an outbreak for a long time, so he never told me about it."

Certainly, if either one of you has been exposed to sexually transmitted diseases, it's important to be tested and have a clean bill of health. Even the "minor" STD's can lead to major problems, especially if they remain undiagnosed and untreated.

Lifestyle choices about eating, smoking, drug use and exercise all have an effect on current and future health. It's not only okay, it's vitally important to talk about those issues if they concern you. If you're afraid to talk to your husband about lifestyle choices, my special report entitled *Caring Confrontation* may help you. See the Resources section on how to get your free copy.

If illness does strike either of you, or your children, it affects both of you dramatically. If your husband gets sick, you will not only be concerned about helping him get well, you will also need to take over his family responsibilities while he is unable to carry them out. You may experience extra financial strain as well.

When you are ill, the situation is reversed: your husband has to handle your responsibilities as well as his own, along with doing whatever he can to take care of you. And if your child is ill, both of you may be under immense strain.

If you need to deal with any kind of illness that lasts more than a day or two, remember that caregivers also need relief. Instead of trying to be strong and do everything by yourself, please ask your family and friends for support, and accept what they offer. This will not only help you, it may also help them realize they can ask for support when they need it.

Affairs Happen When Problems are Ignored

Affairs happen. Pretending that this can never happen to you is sort of like pretending you're invisible when you close your eyes. And if one of you has an affair it does not automatically mean that your marriage is doomed.

Although some women believe that they would immediately divorce a husband who has had an affair, it usually isn't that simple. Even when you feel betrayed, there are many reasons to stay in your marriage: children, finances, religious beliefs, shared property, family, mutual friends, business relationships, and fear of loneliness, to name a few.

I know that marital infidelity is fairly common, but I have a skewed personal sample because many couples seek counseling when one discovers the other has been unfaithful. My search for accurate data led me to think many of the statistics on marital cheating are invented for their shock value. The most reasonable looking numbers I have found show that 22% of men and 14% of women admitted having an affair during their lifetimes.

Other statistics I've seen show that 75% of couples who have affairs eventually divorce. That number seems high to me, because many of the couples I have worked with recognized that the affair was a symptom of problems that they tried to pretend out of existence. Once I helped them start talking about those problems they not only survived their affairs but created much stronger marriages than they had before.

Married people become susceptible to extramarital affairs when they are not receiving the kind of attention and appreciation they want and expect from their spouses. When you let your marriage become routine and focus on all of the things that need to be done instead of on each other, you're asking for trouble.

Couples find lots of good reasons—jobs, money, children, hobbies, friends, housework, the Internet, texting, cars—that they can't spend meaningful time together. Feeling alone and neglected doesn't mean one of you is going to have an affair. But feeling alone and neglected coupled with opportunity (and often alcohol) will definitely increase your risk.

Recovering from an affair and learning to trust again isn't just a matter of time and forgiveness. (And forgiving doesn't mean forgetting.) It takes changing the conditions that led one of you to be unfaithful in the first place. That takes commitment and work that's best done with outside support and/or professional help.

Never Excuse Physical Mistreatment

If you are hit, kicked, pushed, shoved, grabbed, tripped, slapped, cut, slammed or any combination of the above, you need help. No matter what you did, no matter what he says, you do *not* deserve physical mistreatment.

Seek medical attention if you need it, and tell medical professionals the truth about what happened. If you don't, sooner or later the mistreatment will happen again, *no matter what he tells you and no matter what he promises*. Any man who physically mistreats a woman needs help, and the only way he'll get it is if you report what has happened.

If he abuses you, remember that it isn't your fault! It's nothing to be ashamed of! Don't lie about what happened! No matter who tells you that the abuse is okay because he's your husband and you must have done something wrong, remember this:

IT ISN'T YOUR FAULT!!!

If he is remorseful and says he's sorry and begs for your forgiveness and promises to never do it again and brings you flowers and takes you someplace wonderful, you still need help.

Remember, if you forgive him and don't do anything to get help, it will happen again, and next time it will be worse. Abuse is cyclical. He'll be nice for awhile, and then something will happen (or he will make something happen, or imagine that something has happened) that he can use as an excuse for losing control and hurting you again.

You may be reluctant to bring your abuse to the police because you want to protect your spouse's reputation or your economic dependence on him. Remember, your safety is paramount. Before you are in danger, create a plan for a temporary safe haven. It can be a friend's house, a shelter or a motel.

You can start to find help by contacting the National Domestic Violence Hotline at www.thehotline.org

Shocking Surprises Occasionally Occur

Alexandra simply wrote, "I wish I had known that he was gay."

There's no way to prepare for that kind of revelation. Some women who have experienced it have considered it an incredible betrayal. This is another instance where you absolutely need help. Both therapy and support groups will be helpful.

A good resource is http://carolgrever.com/. This author is a survivor of that experience and has written moving and useful books to help you understand and cope with your situation.

Other shocks can happen, and they are also survivable.

Lois, one of the most courageous women I've ever met, learned that her husband was a sex addict. This meant that he had had literally hundreds of brief sexual encounters with other women, both before and during their marriage. Not only was she emotionally devastated by his revelation, she was frightened and appalled by his putting her at such a high risk for contracting sexually transmitted diseases.

Instead of just leaving the marriage, Lois decided to accept the fact that sexual addiction is a disease and to honor her commitment to remain with her husband through sickness and health. With her support and his commitment to overcome the addiction, he entered a treatment program and successfully completed it. When I encountered them again about 15 years later, their marriage had not only survived but had become one of the strongest and most loving relationships I've ever seen.

After much agonizing, Marianne's husband acknowledged that he felt like a woman in a man's body. He went through a successful process of sexual reassignment. Although their marriage ended, Marianne and her former husband remain close friends.

Alexandra, Lois and Marianne didn't attempt to manage these monumental crises alone. They all had professional help and support systems. If you are called upon to face something that feels overwhelming, get the help you need. Remember, you're worth it!

Chapter 8
Getting Married Doesn't Cure Bad Behavior

"I wish I'd known that bad behavior can get worse."

He Changed After We Got Married

Carolyn said, "I expected or thought he was 'this person' and after we were married I found out he was also 'that person' too. Before we were married it was totally awesome, and I thought I had found the perfect man for

Being Married

me. We were in sync. Later, I found he had a totally different way of thinking, of behaving and treating others."

Nancy, 70ish, wishes she had known "that all marriages are not made in Heaven."

Sometimes you get no inkling at all that the man you think you are marrying will behave very differently after you're married, but most of the time there are hints. If you know a man for just a short time, he can usually keep up the pretense of being polite and considerate. Over a longer period of time, though, you have more of a chance to observe small things about his behavior.

It's important to notice whether he observes the boundaries you set. Does he urge you to do things that you've already said you don't particularly enjoy? It could be as simple as urging you to go the basketball game when you've told him you'd rather spend the evening at home, or repeatedly ignoring your restaurant suggestions and instead taking you where he wants to go. Be especially cautious if his evaluation of his ex-wife is very derogatory. She may be very much like you. It's easy to ignore little signals like this or make excuses for them, but it's wise to be wary: they may be samples of his ordinary behavior.

You may not notice these specific signals, but they may activate an intuitive awareness that something is wrong. Julie wishes she had "trusted my subconscious thoughts and feelings about my partner." Several women who said they wished they had waited reported having had this experience.

Occasionally you will be taken in by a deliberately manipulative man who appears charming in every way until after he has essentially trapped you. His behavior changes abruptly, and you are confused and upset, wondering what you did wrong. The answer is, nothing! If this happens to you, I recommend reading Mary Jo Fay's intense book, *When Your Perfect Partner Goes Perfectly Wrong*, as soon as possible. This book can help you decide what to do. (See the Resource Section.)

Being Married

He Doesn't Keep His Agreements

Liz wishes she had known "the signs of a passive-aggressive man."

Heather wishes she had known "how he lives for today and is not future-minded." Of course, she might have been attracted to him in the first place because he was so relaxed and she was so intense.

One morning such a man appeared on my doorstep, without an appointment. He was very bewildered because his frustrated wife of over 40 years had thrown him out of the house the night before. His story was that since his recent retirement his wife wanted him to take over the vacuuming. He had agreed to do so, but somehow he couldn't manage to remember to do it, and when he did vacuum, she never seemed very satisfied with the result. By his report, he had always been an exemplary husband, so he was astonished by his wife's reaction to "this one little thing."

Passive-aggressive behavior is aggression caused by *not doing something* instead of by doing something wrong. It usually happens when somebody (in this case a man, but women are also guilty of this behavior) agrees to do something that he doesn't really want to do. For some reason he doesn't feel as if he can say no or negotiate. He may not even be very aware that he's a little angry about being asked.

He always has a good reason for not getting to whatever it is he agreed to do, like the vacuuming. He doesn't feel angry about it; in fact, he's very laid back or apologetic. Instead you're the one who feels angry, but you think maybe you shouldn't be angry because he has such a good excuse. What you usually say in this situation is, "He's driving me crazy!" You probably say this about your children, too.

It's not the man who is passive-aggressive, it's his behavior. There are a number of different ways to cope with passive-aggressive behavior. One is to set very clear agreements that include the time something will be completed and what will happen if the agreement is not kept. There is an expanded explanation of how to do this in the article "Broken Promises—A Five-Step Plan to Get Your Husband to Keep His Agreements" You will find the link in the Resources Section. Another way to avoid this kind of behavior is to learn how to say no to things you really don't want to do and to encourage your husband to do the same. Then, if neither of you wants to do something, you can either hire someone else to do it or make a joint decision that it doesn't need to be done at all.

If it's not an option to leave it undone, you could decide to do it together, even though you may not want to. When you share a disliked task, at least you have each other's company while you do it, and neither of you needs to feel angry by being stuck with the job. At best, you might actually enjoy working together to get a necessary task taken care of quickly and well, and then celebrating your accomplishment by doing something that's fun for both of you.

Abuse Must Be Named!

Suzanne says, "I wish I had known he was an abuser. That's why I divorced him."

Abusive behavior can be verbal as well as physical. It can be regular and ordinary behavior that a man learned in his own family, or it can occur because of a mood-altering substance like alcohol or drugs. It's usually characterized by the husband blaming the wife for everything, real or imagined, that goes wrong.

Women who grew up in families where anger, blame, sarcasm and putdowns were common may not recognize how destructive it is to live in that kind of situation. When you expect to be treated this way, it doesn't occur to you that anything is wrong. It just seems normal.

Heather says, "A few months after we were married, the whole thing flipped. When the sarcasm and abuse faucet began to drip, I got hooked. I wish I had recognized that I was *addicted* to abuse and had known how to leave. It was *so* subtle and so crazy-making, I didn't know how to speak to it—I thought it was all my fault."

Being Married

Paula tried to escape her abusive mother by being sexually promiscuous. She thought the man she married knew and accepted this about her past. She wishes she had known "that he would punish me for past sexual experiences."

While verbal abuse may not be as dangerous as the physical abuse described in the previous chapter, it is dangerous to your self-esteem and sense of well-being. And it can and often does turn into physical abuse. You need to either find a way to change this situation or leave the marriage.

Sometimes you try to fight verbal abuse with your own verbal defense system. This usually makes it worse. You need help. A counselor, class or support group can help you learn to sort through your own behavior and respond effectively to this kind of attack.

> **You don't deserve this kind of treatment,
> and you can do something about it.**

Mental Illness is Frightening and Frustrating

It's also much more common than many people realize. The World Health Organization (WHO) estimates that 1 in every 4 people develops one or more mental disorders (including addictive disorders) at some time during their lives.

Melanie says, "I wish I knew how to recognize the signs of mental illness and whether or not I felt I could deal with it." And Anna says she wishes she had known about "my ex-husbands mental health issues."

ASHA International www.myasha.org, a very user-friendly website, defines mental illnesses as disorders of the brain that disrupt a person's thinking, feelings, mood, ability to relate to others, and daily functioning. Depression is the most common. You have probably heard of others, such as bipolar disorder, post-traumatic stress disorder (PTSD), and schizophrenia. There are dozens more, and most of them can be treated successfully.

Being Married

The important thing to recognize is that when someone's behavior and/or mood has changed dramatically, it's time to pay attention. Sometimes the change occurs so slowly that you barely notice it happening, until you think back and remember the way it used to be.

Common signs of depression include persistently feeling sad or down, decreased interest in having fun or enjoying sex or doing much of anything, change in weight, too little or too much sleep, feelings of worthlessness or guilt, problems making decisions, and thinking a lot about death or suicide. Every one of those symptoms can cause problems for you when your husband experiences them; however, he may not notice or pay attention to the symptoms. He may tell you nothing is wrong and sincerely believe it, while it's clear to you that there's a problem.

If your husband shows signs of suffering from depression or any other mental disorder, the best thing to do is encourage him to see his doctor or talk to a mental health professional. If he cooperates and follows treatment suggestions, you can probably weather this storm in your marriage. If he refuses to get help, or if his illness is one that proves difficult to treat, your life will be much more difficult.

You'll need support to decide what's best for you to do. Your local Mental Health Association is a good resource. So is counseling for you. Both Melanie and Melissa found it necessary to end their marriages. Remember, you don't need to stay in a situation where someone else's behavior is damaging to you unless you know that something is being done to remedy the problem.

Alcoholism Causes Devastatingly Bad Behavior

Abuse of alcohol destroys more marriages than any other single factor. The biggest problem is that the line between socially encouraged, acceptable alcohol use and alcohol abuse is difficult to define. At first, using alcohol seems like a good way to make life easier, less stressful and more fun. It seems like a great problem solver until the alcohol itself becomes a problem.

A friend and mentor of mine is in her 90s and has been divorced for well over 35 years. This wise woman says she wishes she had known how to tell the difference between a person who chronically overuses alcohol, versus one who drinks regularly but whose overuse of alcohol is only an occasional problem that's easily handled.

Abuse of alcohol leads to deadening of the brain centers responsible for judgment. Lack of judgment leads to all kinds of bad behavior. Lynn wishes she had known "that my husband was not going to be faithful to me...and that he would turn out to be an alcoholic." And Suzanne says simply, "I wish I knew he was a *mean* alcoholic."

For some people, alcohol abuse becomes the disease of alcoholism. Alcoholism is a progressive, addictive disorder that gets worse over time and can be fatal. The alcoholic's life revolves around making sure there is a sufficient supply of alcohol available. Relationships don't count unless they are about supplying or withholding alcohol or recovering from the effects of alcohol abuse.

There are many forms of treatment. Alcoholics Anonymous (AA) is helpful for many people. It is free and almost universally available.

If the disease progresses without treatment, he (or she) will use anyone and anything to ensure a supply of this addictive substance. That means using money meant for rent and food to buy alcohol. And you'll be enlisted to help protect him from the negative aftereffects of the alcohol abuse. You'll be ordered to call his boss and make excuses for him. And you'll be blamed when you can't fix things to his satisfaction or when you beg him not to drink. It's a very ugly picture, and it can happen to anyone.

You may feel that you're to blame and that you should be able to do something to fix the situation, but you can't. Your best source of help is Al-Anon. This organization's purpose is to be a resource for relatives and friends of alcoholics. Look on the Internet for a free meeting near you and go even if you feel scared and ashamed. It really can help.

Marriage Isn't a License for Bullying

Louise is a widow who truly misses her husband. Nevertheless, she says, "I wish I had known that the bad temper he exhibited before we were married wouldn't magically go away after we were married." Ella, an 83-year-old divorced woman I met standing line at the post office with her daughter, wishes she had known that her ex-husband "had such a violent temper." Even so, she stayed married for 27 years.

Although these stories come from women who married generations ago, they are still relevant today. Some men live in a fantasy culture where anger is permitted, admired, and even seen as a way to solve problems. In public, these men may conceal their anger in order to stay out of trouble. In the privacy of their own homes, however, they feel freer to demonstrate their power by expressing angry feelings—especially when they are feeling powerless.

If a man grows up in a family where anger is freely expressed, especially by his own father, he may feel that it's his privilege to rule the household with angry, bullying behavior. In fact, these men may have very few problem-solving and negotiating skills. Anger is the only way they know to get what they want.

Angry speech can also be a form of verbal abuse. It is not your marital duty to allow yourself to be abused. Books and online resources mentioned earlier can help you learn more about protecting yourself from angry, controlling behavior. A counselor can help you learn how to respond quietly and effectively to stop angry behavior and avoid making the situation worse.

Of course, ***your safety must be your first concern.*** If there's any question about your physical safety, take appropriate precautions right away.

Being Married

If this kind of behavior is called to the attention of authorities, your husband may be required to take an anger management course. These courses can be very effective in helping a man learn to behave differently.

His Priorities Don't Include Me

Men are not nearly as aware of other people's needs and feelings as women are. It often doesn't occur to them that what they do has an impact on others.

Suzanne complained, "I wish I had known how his daughter was so important to him. Every time she came to visit, it was as if I never existed." Suzanne never could make her husband understand how unhappy she was about the situation—or, if he did understand, he didn't care. She eventually divorced him.

Ann, a 38-year-old executive wife, wishes she had known what her husband's priorities really were. "Rob says his family is his top priority, but he leaves before the kids get up and doesn't get home until after they're in bed. And even when he's at home, he spends most of his time working on his computer. He says he's doing this to provide security for the family."

Ann was almost ready to serve Rob with divorce papers because she couldn't get through to him. They were excellent candidates for counseling. Rob had developed good listening skills at work, but it hadn't occurred to him to bring those skills home. Through counseling, he learned to listen to Ann's concerns, and he cared enough to change his behavior.

If your husband is doing something that causes a problem for you, try asking him the reason that he's focused on it instead of just begging him to stop. Then tell him the reason you'd like him to do things differently. If he listens, that's great. You can problem-solve together about how to get what each of you needs.

If he doesn't listen, get help. This could be from a friend or from a counselor. If he won't go with you to a counselor, go by yourself. The counselor can teach you new strategies to use and help you decide what to do next.

For a story about how Marilyn found a creative way to get her husband's attention, see my blog post, *Getting the Message*, at http://relationship hq.com/blog/2007/01/getting-the-message/

He's Emotionally Unavailable

Betty Ann shares, "I wish I had realized how physically and emotionally unavailable my husband was going to be, not just to me but to our children as well." With four children she chose to stay in the marriage but reading between the lines about how she wishes she were better educated, I suspect she would have preferred to leave the marriage.

There are usually hints about his emotional unavailability before you get married. You may be attracted to the strong silent type because he seems capable of taking care of you and you don't believe you can take care of yourself.

It's only later when you discover that the flipside of this strength, his failure to share his emotions, is not really what you wanted.

Once while teaching a workshop for couples, I heard a woman ask her husband to please share his feelings with her. Her husband responded that he'd be glad to do so, but he often didn't know what his feelings were for a week or two. Most of the men in the room nodded vigorously. I suspect that most of the women were as surprised as I was.

If your husband is like these men, it doesn't help to pressure him to do something he doesn't know how to do. He'll have to learn gradually. A good place to begin is with the questions that are conversation-starters in the *Being Happy Together* book listed in the resources.

Should I Stay or Should I Leave?

This is a tough question to answer. If you are being abused and there doesn't seem to be any hope of correcting the situation, leaving is probably your best option. But as you know, many factors are involved before you make such a choice.

This is especially true if your leaving is likely to infuriate your husband to the point that he tries to harm you physically. Some men are so threatened by the idea of being abandoned that they threaten suicide and/or homicide. Take those threats seriously and get protection. That may mean going to a safe house for assistance. It may even mean relocating to a different city. Your safety is worth it.

Here are three different perspectives about leaving a marriage that is just unsatisfying.

Carolyn, in her early 40s, says, "I love my husband dearly, don't get me wrong, but there was a side to him I didn't know existed. Although we made it through, it was just totally devastating and heartbreaking."

Juanita shares this perspective from her late 70s. "It is worse to be lonely in a marriage than it is to be all alone as a single person without any family at all."

And from a woman recently widowed after a 54-year marriage, who overheard a conversation about this book in while standing in line at the post office: "Death erases and removes all faults and flaws."

Only you can decide whether to stay or go, but secrecy is your enemy. Let people who care about you, and/or professional advisors, help you think through your options. Then make your own decision.

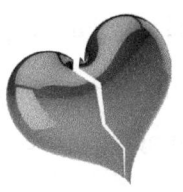

Chapter 9
Stay Conscious About Money

"I wish I'd paid a lot more attention to money."

According to a recent survey conducted by the American Psychological Association almost three-quarters of Americans named money as the number-one source of stress in their lives. If you don't pay attention to money, you're asking for trouble.

It's Best to Share Financial Responsibility

Joyce Asmus shares this comprehensive advice from the perspective of watching her friends get into financial trouble:

"Money will always be an area of conflict. You both have different styles where spending vs. saving is concerned. You must face this before you share accounts and bills, and work with a professional to iron your differences out.

"This is particularly important if one or both of you spends more than you make, is behind on bills, or has a lot of debt. In many states, community property laws dictate that debts as well as assets are shared equally by both partners.

"Don't wreck your credit by taking on his liability! And don't wreck his credit with your liabilities! If you work together to pay off debts and become solvent *before* you say "I do," it will save you a ton of heartache and poverty later!"

Lisa, from the perspective of one brief marriage as a young woman and a second 25-year successful marriage, shares this: "You need to talk about money and be on the same page about each decision, whether it is paying cash for purchases or saving for retirement."

Every couple that follows this advice avoids an incredible amount of grief. But it's much harder than it sounds. Most people find it even harder to talk about money than to talk about sex. We often would rather pretend the whole subject didn't exist, yet it permeates nearly every aspect of our lives. Even the media is filled with advice and conflict about both public and private choices around using money.

Different Values Make Sharing a Challenge

Heather wishes she had known about "his lack of value about savings and communication." And Lisa warns, "What happens when you are dating (frugality, meanness) is amplified after marriage."

Every kind of difference between the two of you can create a challenge to combining your financial lives.

- Your families have different values about money, and quite often one of those values is that money should never be discussed.

- You have different life experiences with money, especially if one of you earns a lot more than the other.

- You have different money personalities. *The Money Couple* identifies five: the savers, the spenders, the risk-takers, the security-seekers, and the flyers. http://the moneycouple.com

When your personal belief systems about money come into the picture, the challenge of sharing responsibility about money can seem insurmountable.

- You tend to confuse your personal worth with your financial worth.

- You tend to judge others based on how they relate to money—and this includes your future husband, even though the judgment is often saved until after the honeymoon.

- You're afraid that everyone who's trying to give you information about money just wants to rip you off.

- One or both of you believes in magic—that if only you could find the right key (job, lottery ticket, stock, get-rich-quick scheme) all your money problems would be over.

- You believe it's your husband's job to handle all the finances.

- In money as in everything else, you believe deep down that everybody is, or should be, exactly like you.

On top of this, one or both of you may believe that money matters are too hard, too complicated, too scary, or too boring—so you refuse to pay attention to them.

Unfortunately, yielding to your discomfort about facing money issues together will just make it worse when the proverbial waste hits the fan—and it will.

In the meantime, any of those barriers can cause you and your husband to become one of the many couples whose number-one area of disagreement is money, especially during the early years of marriage.

Sharing Responsibility Means Sharing Power

When at least one of you believes that the golden rule means "he who has the gold makes the rules," then money is about power in your relationship.

Susan says, "In my first marriage, I had no money or control over family finances. That led to some definite attitudes on my part about money. It's very important that I have my own money, as well as control over how I spend it. I'm happy to share in common expenses, but I would never just pool my money with a spouse."

If you aren't paying the bills, you don't know where the money goes. If you put your paycheck into a joint account and your husband manages the finances from that point on, you may feel as if he's taking care of you… until he suggests that you're spending too much on something, like your clothes.

When this happens, you start to feel as if you must account for every dollar you spend. Before long, you feel as if your spouse controls your life, whether he intends to or not. In any case, you have to hoard cash in order to have any privacy at all about what you spend. It's definitely a recipe for resentment.

You don't have to actually write the checks in order to share financial responsibility and power. Like me, you may not enjoy operating the computer program your husband uses to print checks or pay the bills online. I am very grateful to be relieved of that chore. My husband has chosen to take on the role of bookkeeper in the family, but this doesn't mean he is solely responsible for making the decisions about which bills to pay or when to pay them. We share that responsibility. And we definitely share the responsibility for making decisions about major expenditures. You can, too.

Of course, you could alternate the bookkeeping responsibilities by the month or by the year. Or you could take them on yourself. It doesn't really matter as long as you share responsibility for making financial decisions.

It's up to you as a couple to decide on the mechanics of how you will share financial responsibilities. You can set aside time weekly or monthly to look at your finances together. You can review the checkbook regularly. You can open the mail and review it before you pass it on to him. You can look at bank statements or charge card statements, make notations, and ask questions.

Finding a way to share the power of money is definitely worth it.

Sometimes Deception is an Issue

Whether or not deception is an issue, it's important to share financial information before you get married. Author and former financial advisor Judith Briles put it very bluntly. Her advice is to "check your fiancé's credit report." A credit report gives you a good overall picture of his habits and also specific information about things like payments missed and number of credit cards.

Reciprocity is very appropriate here. It's clearly a case of "you show me yours and I'll show you mine." Not only does doing this avoid unpleasant surprises later, it also gives both of you a chance to correct any errors and improve your individual credit scores before you marry. (Check the bibliography for Judith's book.)

Deliberate deception is a real possibility if your husband-to-be takes the position that his financial information is none of your business. His attempt to maintain financial control could be masked by saying something like, "You don't need to worry about that."

Claire wishes she had known "whether my husband had any debts and how much they were." She also wishes she had had information about his "priorities about expenditures, division of funds and bank accounts if and when both partners are earning, and his assumptions about respective financial responsibilities if or when there are children."

Of course, there are lots of other reasons why either you or your husband might want to keep financial expenditures a secret. They all come down to one of you doing something you don't want the other to know about. It could be something fun, like wanting to create a surprise gift. Or it could be something you're ashamed of, like paying a fine for a traffic ticket.

It could also be something potentially very damaging to your marriage. Jason didn't want Marilyn to see his credit card statements because they reflected the charges for hotel rooms where he had spent time with his mistress. Duane, a gambling addict, definitely didn't want Louise to see their bank balance.

Practicing full disclosure from the beginning at least lets you know about problems as they are occurring.

Being Married

Lack of Skill Causes Problems

Lynn, whose husband turned out to be an alcoholic, wishes she had known "how to manage money!!!!"

There are lots of reasons any woman needs to know how to manage money. Even in the most stable and loving marriage, "stuff happens." Your husband might be unavailable because of illness, accident, extended travel, other responsibilities, or even death, and you'll need to know how to take over the reins. Besides, you can't really be a full partner in your own marriage unless you can contribute to making important financial decisions.

Nobody is born with money management skills. Some lucky people learn those skills from parents who gave them gradually increasing responsibility for handling their own finances from the time they were quite young. But if that wasn't you, don't despair. It's never too late to learn. Best of all, there's a nearly infinite variety of places to get this information.

When I entered "learn basic money management skills" in Google, I got about 6,140,000 results in 0.23 seconds.

Amazon.com turned up 97 books in response to the same words. Of course, that doesn't even begin to talk about the many kinds of classes you can find at your local junior college or adult education center.

You could be overwhelmed with choices if you tried to choose the very best thing to help you learn to manage money. Instead, I suggest that you start anywhere. Choose one thing and get started. If you're having trouble with what you have chosen, discarded it and choose something else. There's no rule here that says you need to finish what you start. For a risk-free investment in your own learning and your future, just explore your local public library. The important thing is to start. Just do it.

Keep Your Own Financial Independence

Nancy wishes she had known that "even if she's married, a woman needs to figure out how to support herself ... and others." And Roberta wishes she had known that it was important to keep her own identity and her own credit rating.

Being Married

In today's uncertain world, you never know when you might be called upon to support yourself and your family. Up to 50% of marriages in the US end in divorce. That's actually a misleading statistic: the risk of divorce varies a lot, based on the length of the marriage as well as the education and wealth of the couple. It certainly doesn't mean that in any given year your marriage has a 50% chance of ending in divorce; however, it does mean that statistically speaking, any marriage is at risk, including yours.

Ruth advises, "Have a separate bank account, for several reasons. So many women pool their money [with their spouse's] and in the event of a husband's death, they're stuck until the will is probated. Also, in the event of a divorce, everything they worked for is long forgotten."

Far too many of my clients stayed in destructive marriages for longer than they wanted to because they were financially dependent on their husbands. Others divorced and were awarded child-support that never materialized. They needed to find a way to support themselves and their children.

Twice-divorced Melanie, who supported not only her son but also both of her deadbeat husbands, is a successful entrepreneur. She says, "I'm proud of the things I've done on my own, without a mate."

Knowing that you can support yourself gives a huge boost to your own self-esteem, as well as providing a safety net for you and your family. This doesn't mean you can't stay home with your children while your husband works to support the family. If you can manage that, it's wonderful. What it does mean is that even though you're at home, you should maintain or improve your job skills instead of thinking you'll never use them again. It's more about attitude than it is about any particular way of doing things.

Being Married

Learn to Communicate about Finances

Amy is very emphatic about this: "Talk about finances and money! Don't assume that how you keep your checkbook and credit will be agreeable to your new financial partner."

Betty Ann says, "I wish I would have known to take control of the finances from day one. We would have been in a better situation financially because I was by nature a good saver. Instead of taking control of the bills and putting my good money sense to use, I assumed my husband was as good at saving as I was and just let him take over. He got the bills paid all right, but we never seemed to have anything much left over. Only later did I realize how much he was spending on items for himself. It really added up. I should have trusted myself more."

One way to start communicating about money is to participate in premarital counseling. That worked for Madonna, who says, "Premarital counseling was helpful. I would say the most important thing it revealed to us was who should handle the finances."

If you think "communication" means talking to each other, you're only partially correct. The part of communication that most people leave out is "listening," which is even more important. Most of the couples I see who have communication problems really have listening problems.

There are two main kinds of listening problems. The first is thinking you understand the meaning of what your husband has said, and vice versa. In financial communication he might say a restaurant is reasonably priced. You think that means about $15 for an entrée. You don't think to question him about what he means because you think you understand. When you arrive at the restaurant and discover that the average entrée price is $25, you're likely to get angry because he lied to you. He didn't. He simply spends time in large cities where $25 is a reasonable price, and that is what he meant when he said reasonable.

The second kind of listening problem is hearing the first few words of what he says, disagreeing, and then focusing your attention on how you'll defend your point of view when he stops talking. When you do this, you miss out on most of what he's trying to communicate.

When communicating about money, it's absolutely critical for both of you to listen, clarify, and be certain you understand your partner's position. Then you can discuss the critical issues of saving, spending, credit, insurance, bookkeeping, decision-making and sharing responsibilities.

The *Being Happy Together* book has 12 different activities you can do separately and together to help you clarify these issues. Check the Resources section for this and other useful material.

His, Hers, and Ours

I'm talking about bank accounts, not children. In a fast-moving discussion about things women wish they knew, all five women present agreed with this point: "You should both have your own money as well as having money together."

My husband and I reached this conclusion when we had been married for about three years and finally had a little bit of discretionary income. (When we married he was in graduate school receiving a small stipend, I was the family wage earner, and we pooled our resources.) I noticed that he was spending almost all the extra income on camera equipment. By this time I knew that our styles were very different: he made decisions quickly, and I tended to take my time. And by the time I had taken my time, the extra money was gone.

I proposed that we take some of the extra money and divide it equally into personal allowances. That worked for us. Over the years the system has continued to evolve. More than 45 years later we still pool most of our resources and maintain personal accounts as well. One thing hasn't changed: he spends most of his personal money, and I invest part of mine. I spend what I like and have a reserve that helps me feel financially secure.

There are many different ways to arrange His, Hers, and Ours accounts. Some couples each contribute part of their paychecks to a shared household account and keep the rest to cover their personal expenses. This works fairly well when their incomes are approximately equal. When one earns substantially more than the other, or if one is a stay-at-home parent, the system we created might be more appropriate.

This is the place to use your financial communication skills to help you figure out what's right for you.

Planning Your Future Includes Retirement

Sharon, 64, wishes that she had been more active in managing her family finances. For years she focused her attention on raising children, on contributing to her church, and on her job as an elementary school teacher. Her husband comfortably and capably took on the role of financial manager.

He hasn't been very communicative about finances, though, and she wonders whether or not she can safely retire from teaching. She convinced him to accompany her to see a financial planner, who sent them home to gather information about their spending habits and all their financial resources. A year later, she's still trying to pull the information together. He has been cooperative about giving her access to most of the records but insists that she really doesn't need certain information. She still wonders if she'll be able to retire when she's 65 or whether she'll need to keep working indefinitely.

You need to pay attention to your financial future at every stage of your marriage. Unfortunately, many couples consider the future to be next month or, at most, the next vacation. This is doing things backward. It's like filling your jar with pebbles and sand and then wondering why it's so hard to fit in the big rocks. You really need to put the big rocks into the jar first and then fit the smaller ones around them. The big rocks are your major long-term goals.

Once you get clear on the big things you want in your future, you can look at what you need to do in order to create them. When you're newly married, that may mean discussing when you can afford to have children or buy a house. Later, it may mean planning for college expenses.

Somewhere along the line you also need to start discussing your retirement goals and start planning to meet those as well. This may seem completely absurd when you're in your 20s or 30s, but that's really the best time to start. Starting may be as simple as putting as much as you can into your employer's 401(k) plan, after reading and understanding the choices the plan offers.

Talking with a financial planner can be helpful at any time. If either of you is bringing substantial assets or debts to your marriage, it's very important to have the conversation before the wedding. It's best to choose a financial planner the same way you choose any other important professional relationship, by getting recommendations from people you trust and then interviewing several before you make a choice.

Chapter 10
Spiritual and Religious Values are Important

"I wish I'd known that spiritual/religious values are important."

Definitions of Spirituality and Religion

These two words are so nebulous, so often misunderstood, and the cause of so many disagreements, that I have included definitions of them directly from Wikipedia:

Being Married

Spirituality can refer to an ultimate or an alleged immaterial reality; an inner path enabling a person to discover the essence of his/her being; or the "deepest values and meanings by which people live." Spiritual practices, including meditation, prayer and contemplation, are intended to develop an individual's inner life; spiritual experience includes that of connectedness with a larger reality, yielding a more comprehensive self; with other individuals or the human community; with nature or the cosmos; or with the divine realm. Spirituality is often experienced as a source of inspiration or orientation in life. It can encompass belief in immaterial realities or experiences of the immanent or transcendent nature of the world.

Religion is a collection of cultural systems, belief systems, and worldviews that establishes symbols that relate humanity to spirituality and moral values.

By another definition, religion is an attempt by humans to establish contact with a conceptualized and referred higher power. They do this for protection, but also due to a certain degree of fear.

Many religions have narratives, symbols, traditions and sacred histories that are intended to give meaning to life or to explain the origin of life or the universe. They tend to derive morality, ethics, religious laws or a preferred lifestyle from their ideas about the cosmos and human nature.

These definitions are so complex and comprehensive that I'm including another explanation of spirituality that speaks to me personally. This explanation is from the book *Passion for Life* by my late good friends Muriel James and her son, John James.

"A universal hunger pervades the world. It is the hunger to get more out of life, to give more back, to be more involved, and to find more meaning. This is the hunger of the soul searching for 'something more.'

"A passion for life... is the commitment to life that motivates us to do our best to strive to make a positive difference in other peoples' lives. ... It reflects a commitment to be and to do more than we believed was possible."

Being Married

Spirituality is a Perspective

Spirituality, or a sense of awe at the immensity and beauty and power we encounter, is an experience many of us stumble upon and have few words to describe. When another person shares the experience with you—and you both know, without words, that you're sharing it—it brings you closer to each other.

This experience can come from viewing something in nature. It could be a sunset, waves crashing on a beach, a rainbow, a sudden vista of enormous beauty, or any of thousands of other wondrous things. The experience can also come from recognizing the wonder of a newborn baby, whether it is a human baby, a kitten, a calf or a giraffe. Any of these experiences can create the same kind of overpowering awareness of the wonder of the universe.

Many religions have been created when individuals have had powerful spiritual revelations that caused them to take a position of leadership in the world as they tried to share their experiences with others. The religious rites attempt to create a place where others can awaken their own spiritual awareness. Many people experience a sense of awe when they practice the rituals of their own religion.

Some persons regard these religious rites as mere formalities they must practice. For them, the rites are associated with a negative rather than a positive emotional experience. Others have learned to believe that they belong to the only true religion and that it's their job to spread that information to the world. Both of these situations can cause conflict rather than a sense of connection—especially when one member of a couple is passionate about something that the other member experiences negatively.

Spiritual Value Definitions Differ

Sara wishes she had known about her husband's spiritual and religious values.

Being Married

Depending on your age when you marry, you may not know much about those values yourself. You may have dutifully attended religious services and followed (or rebelled against) the rules you were expected to follow. You may never have given much thought to why those rules existed. It's only when you're older that you begin to really question or understand the value system you have been following.

Indeed, many spiritual and religious traditions are based on a series of instructions about how to be in the world. Some families focus strongly on raising their children to follow a certain set of instructions. They may talk about the instructions and the reasons for following them. Other families simply teach their children to be good, with good being whatever parents happen to value. When children reach adolescence they may encounter or actively search for instructions that are different from those they were exposed to earlier.

When we're relaxed, happy and thinking rationally, we're more likely to follow the rules we chose when we were adolescents. When we're stressed, we may automatically go back to our original family rules. This double system creates a lot of confusion for many couples, especially when they're young and involved in developing their careers and families. It's only later, after their careers and families are established, that they may begin to search for meaning in their lives.

This search often takes place when you're in your 40s. In fact, many religions don't allow you to study "the mysteries" until you reach that age. So many systems of study are now available that it's hard to choose. As one of those seekers, I spent many days in workshops with wonderful teachers and filled at least three bookshelves, simply exploring without quite knowing what I was looking for.

Spirituality and Religion Help Explain Experiences

At some point many of us address several important questions. What does my life mean? Why am I here?

BEING MARRIED

What am I supposed to do? For some people the answers are part of a religious system we have been taught since childhood. Others search more or less randomly for answers.

Most of us find comfort when we are part of a bigger group. We're looking for which group has the best explanation of why we fit into it. Accepting the values of the group helps us make choices about how to express what's important to us.

Even groups such as Boy Scouts and Girl Scouts, with their motto of "do a good deed every day," contribute to our spiritual development. Practicing random acts of kindness, embracing the seven spiritual laws of success, attending drum circles, learning the *Tao of Pooh*, learning Buddhist meditation practices, studying *A Course in Miracles*, walking a labyrinth, and an infinite number of other things help us in our search for meaning.

Contributing our labor to building homes for needy people, cleaning up our neighborhoods, volunteering to help someone learn a new language or new skill, organizing the church study group, preparing meals for shut-ins, can all be ways of expressing the meaning that we find.

You and your husband may choose to contribute time or resources, together or separately, as a way of expressing your spiritual values in the world.

Spirituality and Religion Provide Community Support

Vivian told me, "I wish we would have been Christians before we got married." When I asked her how that would have made things different, she replied, "We would have had more fellowship and interaction and support from the church people."

Regular interaction with a group that both values you and shares your values can help you feel secure and happy. Members of that group can also help you get through the inevitable rough times in your life and in your marriage. And the stories you tell each other in the group help you affirm that life has meaning.

Being Married

On some level we all know that we need to belong to a tribe. Since most of us live in nuclear families that are separated from our extended families, we need to create this tribal experience for ourselves. Sometimes it happens spontaneously. One couple described the wonderful ritual of having brunch after church with the same group of families once a month for 20 years. The group started spontaneously and has served as a wonderful support for all its members.

Other groups are organized by a religious or spiritual organization specifically to provide this kind of support. And still others are started by one or two individuals who recruit others who seem to share their values system, in order to have a place to discuss those values and how to apply them in the world.

You might want to seek or start such a group to help you share and further develop your spirituality and values as a couple.

Differences in Values Create Tension

Anita wishes she had known about "the importance of mutual participation in religion/spiritual avenues."

When you're in love, the fact that you have different values about participating in religious and spiritual activities doesn't seem very important. If one of you goes to church regularly, you just continue to do what you've always done and don't get together that day until later.

Once you're married, though, you may become a little resentful when he doesn't want to accompany you to church, because in your belief system married couples go to church together. In his family, Sunday morning was a time to hang out in your pajamas and read the newspaper, and he thinks going to church is a waste of time.

If you come from very different religious traditions you may be aware that you will have to sort some things out when you have children, but this seems so far in the distance that you're sure you'll be able to figure it out when it happens. Right now you can just respect each other's practices.

Being Married

If you make regular contributions to charity or volunteer to help a nonprofit organization, you may unconsciously expect your husband to join in these activities after you're married. He may have other ideas.

You may also discover that your feelings about the situation change once you're married. You can't know how attached you are to the nearly unconscious expectations you have about what marriage is supposed to be like until those expectations aren't met.

It's best to have serious conversations about these potential problems before you marry. You need to take into account what each of you feels is important and why. The "why" is very important here. Once you explore the reasons that something is important to you, you may be able to create a new practice that will work for both of you.

Even if you have these conversations before you marry, you may need to have them over and over again later. Your needs for religious or spiritual practices and support will change as your marriage develops.

You can find information about the stages of relationship development in this series in *Being Happy Together: What to Do to Keep Love Alive.*

Some People Search for Spiritual Engagement

Cynthia eloquently states the impact of missing this critical support. "I wish I had truly known I was loved by God, instead of thinking I somehow didn't qualify, which made me very angry. (Otherwise why would I have been given parents who didn't really want to be parents and made the lives of their children utterly miserable?) If I had truly known I was loved by God, I would have believed I was loveable instead of thinking I was just an angry bitch whose husband was stupid for loving her.

"In the same vein, knowing I was truly a good person might have given me the confidence to become a parent. I didn't because I believed I would be the same as my own parents and I didn't want to make another child as unhappy as I had been. I am finding now at age 56 that being childless is a very large empty space which I see so filled in the lives of my friends and colleagues."

If you are as wounded as Cynthia, you need to seek your own healing. Often support groups for adult children of alcoholics can help with these issues. But even that may not be enough. As a psychotherapist working with deeply wounded clients, I found that a combination of psychological and spiritual techniques is often needed for healing.

Often people I worked with hoped that God would heal their pain without the necessity of engaging in sometimes painful psychological work. Although such healings may happen under some circumstances, I have never observed this kind of miracle. Instead, doing the psychological work seemed to pave the way for their acceptance of spiritual experiences.

In the Resources section I've listed several of my own books that address healing your wounded inner child.

Selfishness Undercuts Spiritual Connection

"Some of the biggest challenges in relationships come from the fact that most people enter a relationship in order to get something: They're trying to find someone who's going to make them feel good. In reality, the only way a relationship will last is if you see your relationship as a place that you go to give, and not a place you go to take."

—Anthony Robbins

When you grow up surrounded by a competitive belief system that says there are winners and losers in every aspect of life, you usually figure out which category you belong in. Winners often believe that the way to win is to take from the losers. Losers often believe that they are victims and entitled to take anything they can get from the winners.

It doesn't matter whether winners marry winners, losers marry losers or winners marry losers. When they're stuck

Being Married

in a competitive belief system, everyone in the relationship loses because everyone approaches the relationship from a position of "what's in it for me?" The problem isn't necessarily with the individuals who were involved. The problem is with the system that fosters competition.

One of the biggest challenges in a relationship is to learn to cooperate instead of compete. It can be broken down into a simple formula that many couples have used to meet this challenge.

Here's the formula. Every time you need to make a choice or decision, make sure you take three things into account:

- Your own needs and feelings about the decision
- The other person's needs and feelings about the decision
- The resources and limitations present in your environment

When you practice this approach you learn that giving and receiving are part of the same system and each has its own rewards.

Using Marriage for Spiritual Growth

This happens only with couples who both talk about and actively practice values that reflect a passion for life. These couples have goals that are based upon their values. When you are in this kind of marriage, the choices you make include the added dimension of whether they move you closer to or farther away from your goals.

You "put your money where your mouth is" by using your time, your energy and/or your money to work with others to help achieve these goals. Sometimes this involves doing something alone, sometimes it involves doing something together, and sometimes it involves one of you providing support and backup so the other can make the active contribution.

If your value is to help those who are less fortunate than you are, you might volunteer to work with an organization like Habitat for Humanity and help build affordable homes in your own community. You might volunteer to spend your vacation on a church mission trip to provide aid in an undeveloped country. Or you might volunteer at a shelter for homeless people.

If your value is helping children, you might serve as foster parents, volunteer at the PTO, become a storyteller at the library, or work together to create a playground. You could help create a scholarship fund or serve on the board of a nonprofit organization that serves children.

If you value public service, you might serve on a citizens' committee in your own community, work together on a political campaign, or even run for public office with the support of your spouse.

If environmental issues are your passion, you can join others involved in building trails, planting flowers, creating parks, or finding ways to recycle anything from used medical equipment to automobile tires.

Start anywhere. The possibilities are endless, and so are the rewards.

Chapter 11
Secrets that Make Marriage Work

*"I wish I'd known what it really takes to
makes a marriage work: giving up the myths."*

It Really Takes Hard Work

"Marriage is the hardest job you will ever have! It takes a lot of WORK, day after day, conflict after conflict, drudge after drudge. Interspersed with that reality are some really rewarding times, and some of the most stressful times too. You have to be ready for the drudgery so that you can really appreciate the wonderful times.

Being Married

"And you have to understand that successful marriages are built on the understanding that the bond the two of you forge makes you MUCH more than the sum of your parts. Nothing can stop two people who are totally committed to each other from reaching their goals and dreams!"

—*Joyce Asmus*

Paula has been happily remarried for 32 years, after two unsuccessful marriages. During a couple's group discussion, she shared what made her third marriage last: "Once you are married, you have to take the other person into account for it to succeed." One of the men present agreed. He added, "You have to learn to handle things you would have walked away from before the marriage."

It's a real challenge to confront the fairytale myth of "getting married and living happily ever after." Too many women think it's supposed to be easy, and when it isn't, they start to question whether they've chosen the wrong man.

Heather wishes she had known "the incredible amount of work it takes every day to stay emotionally, mentally, sexually, and spiritually connected and maintain intimacy!" And Anita recognizes the time it takes to do that work. She wishes she had known "how demanding marriage is on time."

Being willing to commit the time and energy to make a marriage work may be more important than finding your perfect soulmate. And even if you are married to your soulmate, you'll still need to do the work involved if you want to have a successful marriage.

Breaking the Codependency is Very Challenging

Ruth describes how easy it is to get into a situation where you both agree that the needs of one of you are more important than the needs of the other. "In the honeymoon glow, most wives turn cartwheels trying to prove what wonderful wives they are."

Being Married

Then she describes how to avoid the problem in the first place: "I wish women could be told to ask the new hubby, right from the start, to do some of the chores she will later expect of him. Men get spoiled and then assume that's how it will always be."

It is much more comfortable to be the one in the relationship whose needs are more important. Throughout the history of Western civilization, men were considered to be more important than women, who were expected to serve the men they married. It is only within the past century or so that this notion has been questioned, and many men still seem to think that's how things should be. So it's usually the woman, you, who is the first one to get uncomfortable in a codependent situation.

Codependency really isn't good for either of you. Unfortunately, both of you have been so exposed to the idea that marriages are supposed to be codependent, it's hard to relate in any other way at first. Gloria wishes she had known "that my marriage is unique and has nothing to do with anybody else's marriage, especially my parent's marriage."

Julie wishes she had known "that marriages can change over time, as partners mature." Actually, no truly satisfying relationship is static. Relationships do grow and change over time. Apparently by nature's design, the intoxication of falling in love lasts at least long enough to get babies started (it's those "selfish genes" again.) Once the honeymoon is over, the real work of creating a mature and loving relationship can get started.

To grow that kind of a relationship, Amy offers this advice she wishes someone had given her: "Have together lives and separate lives. Couples shouldn't have to be attached at the hip all the time. It is important to set up rules of engagement when it comes to having "me time" which everybody (whether they think so or not) needs!"

BEING MARRIED

You Can't Complete Each Other

In a codependent relationship, you each take on the responsibility of making up for anything your partner lacks. This means if he can't stand cooking, you do it. It also means that if you are afraid of driving in traffic; he'll do that for you. Your relationship is based on needing each other.

Barbara wishes she had known "that it would take two people working together. I wish I had known it would not be enough for me to do all the flexing and pleasing to come to resolutions."

At first, you're each thrilled to have someone who needs you. Later, you are likely to become resentful about it. Each of you may feel that the situation is one-sided, that you're the one who is sacrificing for the other.

Dana wishes she had known that "trying to complete each other is a bad idea." You can't really do it. And even if you could, it creates a fantasy that each one of you is incapable and incomplete. If you keep believing you (or your husband) can't really do something, you never try, you don't get any practice, and eventually it becomes a self-fulfilling prophecy.

You become a grown-up person who believes you are incapable of functioning in the world by yourself. You can't balance a checkbook, you can't cook, you can't read a map, you can't make social engagements, you can't hold a job, you can't change a diaper, you can't express sympathy, and a whole variety of other "cant's" that have nothing to do with what either of you could learn to do if you needed to. It's really a way of dishonoring yourself and your partner.

Eventually you get uncomfortable enough in a codependent situation that you decide you want to be a whole person, regardless of what you think you're supposed to be doing. At this point, a lot of women think the only solution is divorce. It isn't.

Edith reports, "I wish I had realized that life will present tough issues, and when you honor yourselves you will get through them better." Honoring yourself and each other means to stop trying to complete each other and instead to support each other in becoming two separate individuals who are complete in themselves.

You're Two Different People

Lynn wishes she had known "that I would actually have a life of my own after the kids were raised; I came into my own in my 40's and started my design business. That it's okay to want something for yourself."

When you finally reach the point of recognizing that you really are an individual, even though you are married, you may be excited or dismayed. Alicia, who had been a stay-at-home mom for 15 years, stood up in a workshop and said, "I have needs of my own! I don't know exactly what they are, but now I know I'm going to find out."

Linda wishes she had known "that we are different but still can love and respect each other." That can be an exciting revelation.

In my own marriage, I was relieved to discover that it was okay to be different. I thought there was something wrong with me because I couldn't seem to squelch the part of me that valued classical music and ballet over jazz and hockey—my husband's preferences. Once we acknowledged our differences we were able to problem-solve about how to manage them.

One of our solutions involved each of us taking responsibility for inviting the other to join us at our favorite events—and feeling free to accept or decline such invitations. So now, instead of complaining or feeling resentful when I join him at a hockey game, I can enjoy the parts of it I really do enjoy and be confident that my turn would come.

If you and your husband discover that, like us, your likes and dislikes are very different, your challenge is then to develop your negotiating skills.

Being Married

You Can't Make Each Other Happy

Alice, preparing for her second marriage, wishes she had known "that I am not responsible for his happiness and he is not responsible for my happiness." She also wishes she had known "it is not his job to fulfill my needs."

If you're not responsible for each other's happiness, then you each can take responsibility for your own happiness. It's much easier that way. Knowing that you're not responsible for your husband's happiness relieves you of the anxiety that many women feel about doing an impossible job incorrectly. And it frees up time and energy for taking care of yourself.

Alicia wishes she had known that she was responsible for her own happiness. When she finally started to think about her own needs, she realized how isolated she felt. She found a job as a teacher's aide and enjoyed it so much that she eventually became a kindergarten teacher. Now she loves her job and her life.

You can still care about his happiness and he can care about yours. Happy couples care a lot about each other's well-being. They are usually happy to do things that contribute to each other's happiness, but there's a difference: instead of assuming each knows what the other wants, they now talk about it first.

In addition, they have agreed to be honest with each other about what they want and don't want, and about what they are and are not willing to do. This makes it more comfortable to offer things to each other, to ask each other for what they want, and to avoid accepting things they don't want, with no hard feelings, one way or the other.

This is how it works: If you think about something you'd like to do for your husband, you offer to do it. This is not an imposition because of your prior agreement that he will say yes only if it would really please him. If he says yes, you do it. If he declines, you don't. He does the same for you. It's that simple.

If there is something you would like him to do for you, something that would make you happy, you can request that he do it. Again, there is no imposition because the prior agreement is that he can say yes or no, depending on his own inclination. In this case, he can also say "not now" and make arrangements to do it at another time.

Of course, he has the same options that you do: he can offer, request or negotiate. When each of you feels free to ask for what you want, and to say no to offers and requests, you'll both get much more of what you really want and less of what you don't want.

Disagreeing is as Important as Pleasing

Ann wishes she had known that she "really didn't want a doormat." Instead she "wanted someone to stand up to me and not automatically agree with everything."

Couples who are afraid to disagree get into trouble because it's impossible for two different people to always see things the same way. The disagreements are there, and they can become resentments that poison your relationship.

Phyllis was surprised by what sometimes happened when she and her husband disagreed. She shares, "I wish I had known that I wouldn't always like the person I love."

When you're in love, you tend to ignore the differences that come to light when you acknowledge that you are two separate people. Sometimes those differences can be a source of real annoyance. You may even hate something your husband is doing. You may be so angry you don't even want to be around him for a while. But that doesn't mean you don't love him. It just means that at the moment you don't like his *behavior*, which you can then translate very quickly into not liking *him*.

Being in love makes you ignore those differences. It is not the same as loving. Loving means accepting your husband even though you know he is flawed.

Amy advises you to "make sure that the person you marry is willing to agree to disagree. There are many topics and challenges that can come up where there is no real way to be completely on the same page. But both parties being able to come to a compromise and agreeing to it will go a long way."

Disagreeing is a part of marriage. The trick is to learn how to communicate about disagreements in a way that encourages you to continue to love each other.

Disagree Without Being Disagreeable

Yvonne wishes she had known that "just because you are in love doesn't mean you can live with him 24/7. You need to negotiate first."

Negotiation is critical when you disagree. You should have learned how to negotiate when you were a grade-school kid arguing about your bedtime and whether you could watch a TV show—but you probably didn't.

When you are really honest with each other, there will be new disagreements every day. In the early years of marriage these disagreements are usually about physical things like these: Do you make the bed? If so, who is responsible for doing that, and when? Does it matter whether the cap is on the toothpaste, or whether it is squeezed from the bottom or the middle? Who is responsible for taking out the trash, and how often should it be taken out? Does it matter whether the toilet seat is left up or down? Who decides how the thermostat is set? Who has to empty the dishwasher? If something spills, who cleans it up? Who is in charge of the TV remote?

Later, the disagreements can be about money: how much can be spent on what, how much should be saved, where to invest it, and whether that dream vacation is affordable this year. There can also be disagreements about where to live, how weekends should be spent, where the children should go to school, and whether to use vacation time to visit parents who need help.

Being disagreeable when you disagree means using power *or* control in an attempt to get your way. Doing this may work for a while, but it eventually backfires. Then it turns into an unpleasant argument that goes around in circles. By trying to win at someone else's expense, you both wind up as losers. Check the Resources section to learn what to do if this happens to you.

Negotiating is a more productive process. It's about looking for a solution that will satisfy both of you. To negotiate, you need to know and say what you want and why you want it. Then you need to listen to what he wants and why he wants it. The critical question is always *why*—what's the result you expect to get if we take the action you're proposing, and why is that important to you? Once you know why, you can search for solutions that honor both your reasons and his.

It's even okay to agree to do what you don't want to do some of the time because you want him to be happy—as long as he sometimes returns the favor so you'll be happy. Happily married couples care more about creating mutual satisfaction then about proving a point.

Patricia needed these skills even more than she thought she would. She shares, "I wish I'd known that even though I was marrying my true soulmate, there would be gut-wrenching relationship issues ahead. Soulmate status doesn't inoculate against pain and struggle. It does, however, motivate one to work harder to keep the relationship going."

Trust and Respect are Critical

Like mature love, trust and respect develop over time.

Both are related to consistency. Respect is both an attitude and a way of behaving that reflects that attitude. Respect means knowing and appreciating the values and actions of another person. And it means demonstrating your high regard through your own words and actions.

A group of women meeting together agreed that in a marriage, "the most important thing is respect."

Demonstrating respect means never doing or saying anything that implies your spouse is unworthy. It means never verbally insulting each other, either in person or to a third party. It also means lots of other things that you'll discover as you go along.

Gloria wishes she had known "that it's okay to trust! It took me so long to trust my husband that I suffered a lot with all the things I imagined, and with thoughts that came out of mistrust."

Trust means feeling secure that your spouse will always act in ways that demonstrate those values that are important to him and to you. It means knowing that your spouse would never deliberately do anything to hurt you.

It doesn't mean that he will never hurt you. We all do things that have unintended consequences, and we can't know each other's hidden sore spots. You will hurt each other inadvertently, but if you trust and respect each other, you'll say ouch when you're hurt. You'll talk about the hurt and how to fix it. And you'll try to fix it instead of defending yourself because, after all, it was an accident.

Consistently keeping agreements fosters trust. Keeping even simple agreements, like calling when you're going to be a little bit late, can make a difference. And if you can't keep an agreement or want to change an agreement you've made, you must talk to your spouse about it as soon as you possibly can.

Alice wishes she had known "that I could really accept him for what he is."

Even if your husband is trustworthy, if you've been hurt before, it may take a long time to really relax into trusting him. If that's the case, it's important to explain to him that it's not because of his behavior but because of your past experiences. Trust may build very gradually. It's not a process that can be rushed.

The Rewards are Worth It

> *"Life is a journey, not a destination."*
>
> *—Ralph Waldo Emerson*

Marriage is also a journey, not a destination.

Being Married

Getting clear about your priorities helps make your journey easier. My husband and I have been through a lot together, as have many other couples. We decided long ago that our commitment would be to our own and to each other's growth, rather than to the survival of our marriage. Some of the steps have been exciting, some terrifying, some sad, and some amazing beyond our wildest dreams.

Hard work was once valued for the sense of satisfaction that came with it, but lately, it has developed a bad reputation. Building a successful marriage *is* hard work, with frequent built-in rewards along the way. Each success prepares you to take the next step, and there are lots of resources available that can help you make your journey satisfying and rewarding.

Jody Rigsby said this so beautifully that I want to share all her words with you:

I kept hearing that marriage was hard work. I agreed to that, for a while. What I didn't know was that it may be years of hard work and that if your marriage survives the difficult times it will reach a deeper level of friendship, loyalty, and forgiveness that is well worth it. For me, the difficult time lasted 17 years and the last 5 have been well worth it.

We all change, and if you can commit to the other partner through the ebb and flow (not easy at all), then you will find that you can actually lean on each other while at the same time give each other more space to grow mentally, physically and, most importantly, spiritually.

Bon voyage!

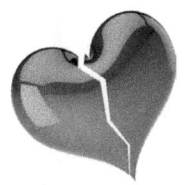

Claim Your Special Bonus Now

If you have not yet downloaded
*A 7-Step Process to Tame the Procrastination Monster
and Learn to Negotiate,* do it now!

www.BooksbyLaurie.com/tame

Please Help Me Reach New Readers

Chances are that you checked out the reviews on this book when you purchased it. Reviews are critical to help prospective readers decide to read books. I would be thrilled if you would leave a review NOW, while you are thinking about it.

If you are someone who has done this before, you know how easy it is.

If you're not, you may be shuddering at the memory of grade school book reviews. This is different!!! Really it is!

Being Married

All you need to do is imagine that you are telling a friend about reading this book. Then follow these steps.

- Say what you would tell your friend into your phone and record it in the notes section and let your phone write it out. (All you need to say is one or two sentences.)

- Email it to yourself.

- Add punctuation if necessary.

- Cut and paste your sentences into a review box wherever you buy your books.

I have included a few links to popular places to leave your reviews. Go to www.BooksbyLaurie.com or www.Goodreads.com/Laurie_Weiss and click on any book title.

I would love to hear from you about how this book impacted you. And, if you have any problems or questions about this book, I would really appreciate hearing from you directly. My email address is Laurie@LaurieWeiss.com. You will find my phone number and social media connections on another page.

Dr. Laurie Weiss

Thank you in advance for taking the time to contribute to the conversation about what to read. I truly appreciate it.

Laurie

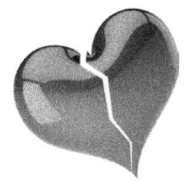

Acknowledgments

This book would not have been possible without the help of many people.

Judith Briles, The Book Sheppard, and my many friends in the Author You community who encouraged me to re-release this book as part of the Secrets of Happy Relationships Series.

Nick Zelinger of NZ Graphics who designed the cover concept and did much more.

Istvan Szabo, Ifj. for both his book formatting skills and his unfailing patience.

My daughter, Rachel Claret, who discovered new places for me to share my work and so much more.

Helen Georgaklis, Founder and CEO of 99 Book Series, Inc. whose vision created the original title of this book and invited me to write it.

My friend Dory Rice, who helped me make the decision to accept Helen's invitation by saying spontaneously, "We'll help you." Dory sparked the idea that this book could be the outgrowth of many conversations with many women.

All of the women who were eager to engage in the conversation and share their wisdom with me and with you.

Ginger Marks, publisher of the 99 Book Series, guided the original development of this book and supported my wish to recreate this version of it.

Donna Jara, my wonderful editor who did much more than edit this book. She taught me the writing and editing skills I've been using for the past 35 years.

And last but certainly not least, my husband and business partner Jonathan B. Weiss for solving my computer problems and putting my data into a form I could work with, for loving me, and for honoring our 50+ year commitment to our own and each other's growth.

Thank you all. I couldn't have done it without you.

Useful Resources

Chapter 1

Laurie Weiss and Jonathan B. Weiss. *Stop Poisoning Your Marriage with These Common Beliefs.* Empowerment Systems Books (2015, 2019)

Easy to read books to help you appreciate how people are different from each other:

> **Enneagram:** Renee Baron and Elizabeth Wagele. *The Enneagram Made Easy: Discover the 9 Types of People.* HarperOne; 1 edition (March 11, 1994)
>
> **Myers-Briggs Type Indicator:** Renee Baron. *What Type Am I? Discover Who You Really Are.* Penguin Books (August 1, 1998)

Very popular description of what makes individuals feel loved:

> Gary Chapman. *The Five Love Languages: How to Express Heartfelt Commitment to Your Mate (new edition).* Northfield Press (2004)

Being Married

Chapter 2

Learn to tell the truth without getting into trouble or losing your friends, by following the stories of people who actually did so. My story is in Chapter 12.

> Laurie Weiss. *What Is the Emperor Wearing? Truth-Telling in Business Relationships.* Butterworth-Heinemann; 22nd edition (February 2, 1998)

Co-Dependency causes enormous distress in marriages. The "Saying No Program" is in Chapter 13.

> Laurie Weiss & Jonathan Weiss. *Recovery from Co-Dependency: It's Never Too Late to Reclaim Your Childhood.* Health Communications, Inc. 1989. iUniverse (June 11, 2001)

There is no longer a need to be embarrassed about subjects you never mastered in school. Lessons available in bite-sized chunks—FREE.

> KahnAcademy http://www.KhanAcademy.org

Chapter 4

Family Communication: Sally Shields. *The Daughter-in-Law Rules: 101 Surefire Ways to Make Friends with Your Mother-In-Law!* Safflower Publishing, Inc. (2008)

Transactional Analysis (TA) is one of the best ways to make sense of how people work. I first learned it in 1965 and it has been the basis of all the rest of my development.

For a very brief basic introduction to TA, search for "Transactional Analysis" at www.youtube.com. I especially like materials created by CounselingTutor.

Muriel James and Dorothy Jongeward. Born To Win: Transactional Analysis With Gestalt Experiments. Da Capo Press; 25 Anv edition (August 30, 1996)

A comprehensive guide to TA. Ian Stewart and Vann Joines. *TA Today: A New Introduction to Transactional Analysis.* Vann Joines (June 1987)

A long-time best seller. Eric Berne. *Games People Play.* New York: Grove Press (1964)

Eric Berne. *What Do You Say After You Say Hello?* New York: Grove Press (1972)

United States of America Transactional Analysis Association www.USATAA.org

International Transactional Analysis Association https://itaaworld.org

Chapter 5

The Secrets of Happy Relationships Series:

    Laurie Weiss. *Relationship Tips for Life Partners.* Empowerment Systems Books (2019)

Being Married

Laurie Weiss. *Being Happy Together: What to Do to Keep Love Alive.* Empowerment Systems Books (2019)

Healing relationships:

Harville Hendrix. *Getting the Love You Want: A Guide for Couples.* Henry Holt & Co; Revised and Updated edition (December 26, 2007)

Harville Hendrix and Helen Hunt. *Receiving Love: Transform Your Relationship by Letting Yourself Be Loved.* Atria (2004)

Chapter 6

Activity to do each week, in an hour or less, to help you grow (or save) your marriage. Laurie Weiss. *Being Happy Together: What to Do to Keep Love Alive.* Empowerment Systems Books (2019)

Chapter 7

Carol Grever. *My Husband is Gay: A Woman's Guide to Surviving the Crisis.* Crossing Press (2001)

If you even suspect that you are being abused: National Domestic Violence Hot Line www.thehotline.org

FREE special report: "Caring Confrontation"
http://www.LaurieWeiss.com

Chapter 8

Mary Jo Fay. *When Your "Perfect Partner" Goes Perfectly Wrong: Loving Or Leaving The Narcissist In Your Life*. Out of the Boxx Pub (2004)

Repairing broken agreements:

>Laurie Weiss. "Getting The Message"
>https://tinyurl.com/yc7qkkka
>
>Laurie Weiss. "Broken Promises—A Five-Step Plan to Get Your Husband to Keep His Agreements"
>https://tinyurl.com/y7ds63py

Very difficult issues:

>ASHA: A source of hope for all touched by mental illness
>http://www.myasha.org
>
>Alcoholics Anonymous www.aa.org
>
>*Al-anon* www.al-anon.alateen.org

Chapter 9

Bringing Love & Money Together: The Money Couple
www.themoneycouple.com

Judith Briles. *Money Smarts for Turbulent Times*. Mile High Press (2009)

Activities about money in your relationship. *Being Happy Together: What to Do to Keep Love Alive*. Empowerment Systems Books (2019)

Chapter 10

BEING MARRIED

Spiritual development from several different viewpoints:

> Helen Schucman. *A Course in Miracles.* New Christian Church of Full Endeavor, Ltd (2005)
>
> Benjamin Hoff. *The Tao of Pooh.* Penguin Books (1983)
>
> John James and Muriel James. *Passion for Life: Psychology and the Human Spirit.* Plume (1992)
>
> Information about The Labyrinth: http://veriditas.org

How relationships change:

Laurie and Jonathan Weiss. *Secrets of Relationship Development* (MP3 Audio)
http://www.empowermentsystems.com/freeaudiolink.htm FREE

Inner Child resources:

> Al-Anon family groups
> http://www.al-anon.alateen.org
>
> Laurie Weiss & Jonathan Weiss. *Recovery from Co-Dependency: It's Never Too Late to Reclaim Your Childhood.* Health Communications (1989) iUniverse (2001)
>
> Laurie Weiss. *Action Plan for Your Inner Child: Parenting Each Other.* Health Communications (1992)
>
> John Bradshaw. *Homecoming: Reclaiming and Championing your Inner Child.* New York: Bantam Books (1990)

Chapter 11

Dr. Laurie Weiss

Laurie Weiss. *Being Happy Together: What to Do to Keep Love Alive.* Empowerment Systems Books (2019)

Special Report: Laurie Weiss. *Dare To Say It: How to Have Important Conversations that Build Working Relationships* (PDF)
www.DareToSayIt.com

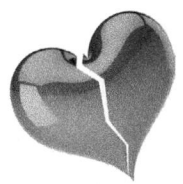

About the Author

Women have been sharing secrets with, Dr. Laurie Weiss for over 45 years. Now she has collected those secrets to share them with you.

Relationship Communication Expert, Dr. Laurie Weiss is internationally known as an expert who helps other relationship consultation professionals develop their skills.

As a psychotherapist, coach, marriage counselor, author and stress relief expert she has helped more than 60,000 individuals reclaim life energy and find joy in life for more than four decades. She has taught professionals in 13 countries and authored eight books that make complex information accessible to anyone. Her latest, ***Letting It Go***, teaches rapid anxiety and stress relief.

www.LaurieWeiss.com

Dr. Laurie is one of only two Master Certified Logosynthesis Practitioners in the United States. She is a Certified Transactional Analysis Trainer with Clinical and Organizational Specialties and a Master Certified Coach. Her work has been translated into German, Chinese, Spanish, French and Portuguese.

She and her husband, Jonathan B. Weiss, Ph.D., started working together in 1970. Both Drs. Weiss love mixing business and pleasure and enjoy visiting professional colleagues and friends around the globe. They live and work in Littleton, Colorado, USA.

Dr. Laurie is passionate about helping people have the important conversations that build great personal and working relationships. She says, "I have an unshakeable belief, based on over 40 years of experience, that people are doing the very best they can with the resources they have available to them at any given moment."

She loves adventures, went indoor skydiving for the first time at age 67 and zip lining for the first time at age 75. She has been blessed by elephants in India, walked on hot coals, visited Camelot, flown over the Pyramids, and spent an afternoon at the sex temples at Khajiraho and learned more possible sex positions than she can possible remember.

E-mail: Laurie@LaurieWeiss.com

Office: 303-794-5379

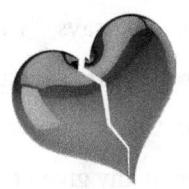

How to Work with Dr. Laurie

My husband, Dr. Jonathan B. Weiss and I have been married since 1960 and business partners since 1972 when we were teaching Transactional Analysis throughout the United States. We have been learning and teaching cutting edge tools for healing and transformation for over 45 years.

We have both been Teaching and Supervising Transactional Analysts for over four decades. Currently we are the only Certified Logosynthesis Practitioners in the United States. Either or both of us would be delighted to help you learn more about creating joy and satisfaction in your life and your important relationships.

Contact Us: We Usually Answer the Phone

You can contact us directly to discuss what is best for you and your group. We offer a variety of options including CLASSES, TALKS, BOOK GROUP VISITS, PROFESSIONAL CONFERENCE PRESENTATIONS, TRAINING, INDIVIDUAL and COUPLES APPOINTMENTS. We work with our clients in person, by phone and by Skype.

Dr. Laurie Weiss:

LaurieWeiss@EmpowermentSystems.com

Dr. Jonathan Weiss:

Weiss@EmpowermentSystems.com

Empowerment Systems

506 West Davies Way

Littleton, CO 80120 USA

303-794-5379

Dr. Laurie Weiss

Websites

Personal – http://www.LaurieWeiss.com

Logosynthesis – http://www.LogosynthesisColorado.com

Business – http://www.EmpowermentSystems.com

Purchase Books – http://www.BooksbyLaurie.com

Social Media

Facebook – https://www.Facebook.com/laurieweiss

LinkedIn – http://www.Linkedin.com/in/laurieweiss

Pinterest – https://www.Pinterest.com/laurieweiss/

Twitter – https://Twitter.com/@LaurieWeiss

Goodreads – https://www.Goodreads.com/Laurie_Weiss

Blogs

Personal Development – http://www.IDontNeedTherapy.com/blog

Relationship – http://RelationshipHQ.com/blog/

Business Communication – http://www.DareToSayIt.com/blog

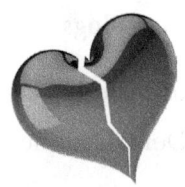

About the Secrets of Happy Relationships Series

Relationships aren't easy. Relationships are often confused and messy with partners trying to find happiness in all the wrong ways.

Real relationships get messy because even though you think your life partner is just like you, he or she isn't. You are two different people trying to meet the challenge of creating and maintaining a happy and loving relationship, perhaps without much useful information.

To make matters worse, you live in the midst of the outmoded role expectations of a culture that values drama and competition and extreme busyness. Most media doesn't help. It focuses on difficult relationships, not successful ones.

Ordinary relationships have their ups and downs and almost nobody writes about those cycles. It's no wonder there are so many misunderstandings. Creating a lasting, loving, growing relationship is an incredible challenge. It's completely natural to have questions about your relationship.

I've been answering questions about relationships since 1973 when I was in newly minted TA (Transactional Analysis) therapist and was sure I had the answers to all the problems of the world. I had been married for 13 years and we had survived some major challenges. I was happily learning and using our new tools. Over four decades later, we are still married and I've learned a lot.

It's been my pleasure and privilege to help people sort out the misconceptions, misunderstandings and challenges of creating happy, loving relationships. Being happy together is a gift my husband and I have given each other through the work of addressing issues as they arise. It's a gift you can have also; by giving it to each other.

Books in the Secrets of Happy Relationships Series

**Are You My Perfect Partner?
To Marry or Not to Marry …**
Are you really ready to get married?

**Being Married:
Secrets Women Wish They Knew**
*Crucial information you need
to know about marriage*

**Stop Poisoning Your Marriage
with These Common Beliefs**
*Are you letting these myths
undermine your marriage?*

Dr. Laurie Weiss

Relationship Tips for Life Partners
Critical guidelines for creating a true partnership

Reconnect to Rescue Your Marriage:
Avoid Divorce and Feel Loved Again
What to do before leaving your troubled marriage

Stop Arguing and Start Talking …
even if you are afraid your only answer is divorce!
Are you ready to have these loving,
productive conversations with your spouse?

Being Happy Together:
What to Do to Keep Love Alive
Unlock secrets to rapid relationship
renewal in just an hour a week

Other Books by Laurie Weiss

Letting It Go: Relieve Anxiety and Toxic Stress in Just a Few Minutes Using Only Words (Rapid Relief with Logosynthesis®)
Are you ready for relaxation to replace anxiety in your life?

Emotional Self-Help: I Don't Need Therapy, But Where Do I Turn for Answers?
Do you need to become emotionally literate?
www.BooksByLaurie.com/answers

**Recovery From CoDependency:
It's Never Too Late To Reclaim Your Childhood**
Are you ready to release your codependency?
www.BooksByLaurie.com/recovery

Dr. Laurie Weiss

**An Action Plan for Your Inner Child:
Parenting Each Other**
Are you ready to reclaim your inner child?
https://www.amazon.com/dp/1558741658

**What Is the Emperor Wearing?
Truth-Telling in Business Relationships**
Do you wish you dared to tell the truth?
www.BooksByLaurie.com/emperor

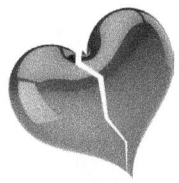

Enjoy this preview of another book in the
Secrets of Happy Relationships series:

Stop Poisoning Your Marriage with These Common Beliefs

Introduction

Interviewer: Hi, everyone. Welcome back to another quick read audiobook, **The Top Ten Hidden Beliefs About Relationships and How to Stop Them from Poisoning Your Marriage**, with Laurie Weiss Ph.D., and Jonathan B. Weiss Ph.D.

Relationship coaches and marriage counselors Doctors Jonathan and Laurie Weiss have spent over 40 years studying, practicing, and teaching relationship-building skills.

They are internationally known coaches, consultants, psychotherapists, speakers, and authors. They have presented their work throughout the United States and in 13 other countries.

Married since 1960, they have been in practice since 1972. They focus on helping clients create dynamic, effective, personal and working relationships.

Now doctors, what should the listeners' number one expectation or outcome be from this audiobook?

Jonathan: To realize that you have the power to create a fabulous relationship starting right now.

Interviewer: Excellent. Let's get started.

Chapter 1
It Takes the Right Person

Interviewer: Hidden Beliefs About Relationships Number One:

If you are with the right person the relationship will work. If it's not working, it must not be the right person. A relationship will only work with the right person.

What exactly is this and what should people do instead?

Laurie: It's actually the belief in soul mates that says there's only one right person out there for you. It's a belief that is wonderful at the beginning but it leads to disappointment, if not panic, when problems come up for the first time.

It may cause people to just decide this is the wrong person, it's time to end the relationship and never even learn to solve problems together.

Jonathan: I think what they need to do instead is to learn to focus on what's really important in the relationship and to talk about it.

Talk about what's desirable, what's truly a deal killer, what they want, and learn how to discuss and solve problems when they come up because they're going to come up. It happens in every relationship and it's not a sign of anything other than they are two different people.

Laurie: The thing is that soul mates are really a myth and every relationship has to be created.

If a marriage is going to last people have to learn the skills and be willing to deal with the kinds of feelings that come up that are not as happy as they were during the courtship.

Jonathan: If they don't do that they're going to get disillusioned, they're going to get angry at the partner for not being the perfect person they thought they were.

They will blame them, they wind up looking outside for somebody better, and they wind up being very vulnerable to having affairs or having serial marriages.

Interviewer: Tell me just a little bit more about this soul mate thing because that's actually something you read a lot about, you hear a lot about, especially on pop psychology-type talk shows and things like that, people talk about their soul mate. What are people trying to accomplish with that?

Jonathan: It's kind of a nice, mystical, romantic idea that there's the perfect person. The truth is that every single person out there has flaws and has strong points, and anybody that you're reasonably attracted to, from our perspective, is somebody that you could work out a really good relationship with using relationship building skills.

Interviewer: Does this mean that, instead of saying that there's only one person out there, there's a certain type of person that is better suited for you than another?

Laurie: I would think that there are a whole variety of people. I wouldn't say that there's a certain type out there, there's just a person that you might hit it off with somewhere.

It might be somebody who's very much like you or it might be somebody whose needs and feelings are very complimentary to yours so that you can take care of them and they can take care of you.

I think one of the main beliefs that people have that gets in the way of marriage is the belief that we are all the same. We are not, we are very, very different.

If you think there's a soul mate, it means that we're already fixed, we're not going to grow, we're not going to change, we are the way we are, and we're perfect for each other. That just isn't true.

Very often people will get married and then what happens is, everything they thought about the other is wonderful, is there, but then something else will show up.

I was working with a client on the phone the other day. This was a second marriage. People generally don't come to us with this kind of problem when it's a first marriage, they just find another one. In the second marriage...

Interviewer: They try again?

Laurie: They find another partner instead of working it through with the first marriage.

Interviewer: Do they typically look for someone completely different than the first marriage or do they end up with someone who's very similar and just repeat the same mistakes?

Laurie: They repeat the same mistake. It's somebody who's wearing a different mask almost. They think, "Oh, this time it will be different. This time I've got the right one" but it doesn't turn out that way.

Jonathan: You have a bunch of criteria for what's going to be a good mate. When you start to form a relationship you're evaluating the other person, sort of testing them and seeing if they match your list, and that kind of thing.

That's a very different procedure and not a very helpful one compared to what can we create together? What is it that together we can do and create that is satisfying to both of us? It's different than testing them to see if they match your standard.

Interviewer: Okay, excellent. Anything else about this that we should be aware of?

Laurie: Well, my client who thought it was perfect, discovered it wasn't, called me when she discovered all the messes her husband had hidden in his closet, and then she worked out a way that she could help him clean up those messes instead of running, which was her first impulse.

Interviewer: So she decided to stay in there and actually work at it this time instead of cutting and running?

Laurie: [affirmative] Mm hmm.

Interviewer: Okay, excellent. Well, let's keep going.

***

You'll find links to all the *Secrets of Happy Relationship Series* books at www.BooksbyLaurie.com. Go there now and order the next book you need to create the happy relationship you want and deserve.

www.ingramcontent.com/pod-product-compliance
Lightning Source LLC
Chambersburg PA
CBHW051531020426
42333CB00016B/1870